"In his book, Chris c ... ...iduals whom he calls *misfi* ... ...ollow God and resist pressure fi ... ...dia. In my years of ministry, I've ... ...who go against the grain end up shaping their culture and influencing their world. As you read this book, I hope you're challenged to join this group of 'misfits' who will impact this generation for the glory of Christ."
Ron Luce, Teen Mania

"Chris Durso lives what he writes and preaches—and that truly sets him apart as a leader in our generation. This book is a must-read for anybody interested in living life as a misfit in a culture demanding conformity. The message in this book is urgent and important."
Carl Lentz, lead pastor, Hillsong New York City

"In *Misfit*, Chris Durso unpacks a truth that not only can save you a lot of heartache, but also can inject a lot of life into your walk with Christ. Recognizing that you're not created 'normal' and that being different is actually a great thing should be very liberating and energizing for all of us. My prayer is that, as you read this book, you'll discover the incredible gifts and talents God has placed in you and thrive like never before."
Dino Rizzo, lead pastor, Healing Place Church

"Christopher bleeds pop culture in a way that very few do—he's an innovator. He doesn't just write about misfits—he is one. And he's blazing a trail right to the heart of this generation."
Rev. Adam Durso, D.D., founder of Youth Explosion Ministries

"In his book, *Misfit*, Chris Durso exhibits his unique ability to speak specifically to the needs of a generation—something that most of today's leaders have been unable to effectively understand or address. His deep insight into the heart of this emerging generation comes from the eye of a true shepherd and will greatly benefit not only teenagers but also those seeking to reach, understand, and impact them."

Dr. Chris Hill, senior pastor, The Potter's House of Denver

"Christopher Durso is a delightful misfit whose voice ennobles others seeking their places in our world. I'm thrilled especially for artists and other creatives to learn from this young man who expresses his faith and creativity in bold and refreshing ways."

Nancy Beach, champion of the arts, Willow Creek Association

"I'm excited about the vision for Chris Durso's book, *Misfit*. God is calling us toward a holy discontent regarding the way things are. And when we fight against the tendency to give in and give up, the world will view us as misfits. So let it be. Vaya, Chris."

Nicky Cruz, Outreach Ministries

"The Bible promises that 'our young men will see visions' (Acts 2:17). *Misfit* reveals the great potential within our young people to influence and affect change. What a challenge for them to make a significant difference in the world without apology."

Rev. Michael Durso, senior pastor, Christ Tabernacle

"*Misfit* is a must-read for youth and young adults in pursuit of greater relationships with God."

Canton Jones

"This book doesn't fit our cookie-cutter, cliché-ridden church culture. That's because Chris is a misfit. Chris has the authority to write this book because he IS this book. Allow it to make you a misfit, too!"

Tim Ross, www.TimRoss.org

"*Misfit* was written for those who believe they don't fit in—or don't want to fit in. If this is you, read this book."
Marty Sampson

"In *Misfit*, Chris Durso takes an authentic look at the tension we experience when we begin to stand out and live beyond the established norm. It's a must-read that will challenge you to accept the fact that you're meant to be different—and to live that way."
Pastor Joe Champion, Celebration Church

"In a world where church attendees often are mistaken for true Christ-followers, Chris Durso brings us words to alert and strengthen us. The Bible says we will be hated by others for the sake of Christ, but we are not to run from rejection or unpopularity. Rather, we should embrace and use our misfit-status as fuel to love our enemies into submission to God's will. Thanks, Chris, for reminding us what this walk is all about."
John Gray

"As the chaplain of the New York Yankees and New Jersey (soon to be Brooklyn) Nets, I'm used to being around playmakers! Misfits are playmakers and game-changers! Misfits are not intimidated by the scoreboard. They see a problem and find a solution. Chris Durso gives us the playbook for becoming a MISFIT! A must-read for anyone who is uncomfortable with the status quo!"
Willie Alfonso, Chaplain of the New York Yankees and New Jersey Nets

MIS FIT

dealing with our God-given discomfort // CHRIS DURSO

*YS youth specialties

ZONDERVAN.com/
AUTHORTRACKER
follow your favorite authors

ZONDERVAN

Misfit
Copyright © 2011 by Chris Durso

YS Youth Specialties is a trademark of YOUTHWORKS!, INCORPORATED and is
registered with the United States Patent and Trademark Office.

This title is also available as a Zondervan ebook. Visit www.zondervan.com/ebooks.

Requests for information should be addressed to:
Zondervan, *Grand Rapids, Michigan* 49530

Library of Congress Cataloging-in-Publication Data
Durso, Chris (Christopher Andrew), 1983-
Misfit: dealing with our God-given discomfort / Chris Durso.
        p. cm.
        ISBN 978-0-310-67117-6 (softcover)
1. Self-confidence—Religious aspects—Christianity. 2. Consolation. 3. Church work with
teenagers. I. Title.
BV4598.23.D87 2011
248.8'3—dc22   2010043543

Cover design: *Studio Gearbox*
Interior design: *David Conn*

Printed in the United States of America

---

11 12 13 14 15 /DCI/ 20 19 18 17 16 15 14 13 12 11 10 9 8 7 6 5 4 3 2 1

I DEDICATE THIS BOOK TO FIVE

very special people in my life: My parents and pastors, Michael and Maria Durso; my best friend, the mother of my children (my babies' momma), my beautiful wife, Yahris; and my two babies, Dylan Christopher and Chloe Hudson—I pray you'll both become everything God wants you to be and carry on the MISFIT torch. I love you both with all my heart.

Thanks to . . .

Mom and Dad for raising me in the way I should walk. You are both amazing models of how to live godly lives. Dad, thank you for praying for me way before I got up every morning. Thank you for showing me how to lead a marriage and be a man. Mom, thank you for praying for me throughout the night, every night. Thank you for never giving up. Your role as a mother was constant, and you never took time off. Thank you for showing me how to pray. Thank you for showing me what characteristics to look for in a wife.

Mom and Dad, you never gave up on me even when doctors said I was too difficult to deal with. Thank you. I love you both more then you will ever know.

Yahris, you have pushed me to work harder and dig deeper than I ever have. Thank you for believing in me and constantly praying for me and lifting me up before God. Your encouragement and cheers do more for me than you realize. When it comes to me living out my calling, you never get in the way, question it, or complain. Thank you. You're an amazing wife, mother, and woman. I am surely blessed. I love you with all my heart.

My brother Adam for passing me the baton.

My brother Jordan for always being there.

My brother Ralph for encouraging me to push the envelope a little further.

My associate Jon Rodriguez for helping me lead Youth Explosion.

Dave Rodriguez for all the late-night and early-morning writing sessions.

My best friend Junior for being a best friend at all times.

Nancy Beach for writing that email to Zondervan!

Every leader, staff member, and teen from Youth Explosion. I love you guys!

Above all, thank you Jesus for this opportunity to represent you publicly, for your salvation, and for your grace. This is all for you. Without you, this book would be meaningless.

CONTENTS

FORE WORD BY JIM CYMBALA

ONE DAY YEARS AGO I WALKED

into the house of a young couple who attended the church I pastor. They were already in leadership positions, and it was evident to our pastoral staff that God's hand was upon them for future involvement in ministry.

Michael and Maria Durso were soon given a wonderful door of opportunity when they were sent out by our church to pastor Christ Tabernacle—a church that has been blessed by God and has grown dramatically over the years. But all that was in the future as I entered their pretty home in Bayside, N.Y., that day.

As I sat at the kitchen table, Christopher was next to me struggling with a homework assignment. His two older brothers, Adam and Jordan, soon came in from the backyard and began pestering Christopher as only older brothers can do. Christopher muttered for them to leave him alone, but it did little to discourage their goal of messing with his peace and quiet.

Suddenly I looked at Christopher and had the strangest sense that this was no ordinary young boy. "Get away from him," I called out. "Leave your brother alone and let him finish his homework." Adam and Jordan meant no harm, of course, but they quickly exited as I came to Christopher's defense.

But it was more than concern over Christopher's homework that moved me to speak that day. I believe God was showing me something about this young man. "Maria," I later said to his mom, "just wait and see how God uses your youngest boy someday." At that point I wasn't aware of all the challenges Christopher was facing, but on that day he became a special person in my heart.

It's now years later, and Christopher is a young married man with two children. My wife and I attended his beautiful wedding ceremony, and the presence of Jesus was there also. I believe Christopher Durso has been raised up by God for the day we live in. He speaks to young people from a unique perspective of vulnerability and total honesty. And his book, *Misfit*, will inspire countless seekers after truth and love to find their answers in the same God who transformed the life of Christopher Durso.

FORE WORD BY HARVEY CAREY

ONE OF MY FAVORITE CHILDHOOD
television shows was *Rudolph the Red-Nosed Reindeer.* Why?
First of all, I loved the Christmas season (and still do).
Growing up in the ghetto, it was the only time of the year
when our neighborhood looked like the nice neighborhoods.
Snow was "no respecter of persons"—it covered the rich and
the poor.

But there were deeper reasons why I was drawn to the
story about the reindeer born with a red nose that left him
ridiculed by and isolated from his peers. I empathized with
Rudolph because I, too, felt as though I didn't fit in when I
was growing up. I loved to read (not popular), my mom was
VERY active in my life (very rare), and I dreamed of changing the world (really out there).

I felt as though I didn't belong.

In one of the Rudolph scenes, he and a band of his peers arrive on a mysterious island inhabited by toys that were different to say the least—a cowboy that rode an ostrich, a train's caboose with square wheels, a water gun that shot jelly, and (my favorite), "Charlie in the Box" (as opposed to Jack in the Box).

They were all misfits; but fortunately, they were ALL misfits. Their collective understanding of their status made their imperfections and unique characteristics not so awkward or unusual.

At one point during my 12-plus years as a youth pastor, the greatest challenge was peer pressure from classmates and kids in the neighborhood. Now through social media, teenagers' worlds have broadened exponentially—yet feelings of isolation and awkwardness are at an all-time high. And still the "I must fit in" merry-go-round is spinning out of control.

How do Christian young people respond to such pressure? How do parents, mentors, and the church rally around our youth and help them understand that their uniqueness— their "misfit-ness"—isn't a curse but a blessing?

When I first met Chris Durso, he shared his passion for "misfits," and it instantly resonated with my heart and soul. Because I've observed many youth ministries preaching a theology that, at its core, is the antithesis to living as a misfit—and not at all reflective of Jesus' message and ministry. As Jesus traveled the world, he was ALWAYS drawn to the marginalized and took great care not only to find them, but also to embrace them. But today it appears our youth ministries, at best, "tolerate" misfits—the ones who don't fit snugly into the culture we tout as the norm. What's more, America's love affair with external beauty, monetary wealth, cultural elitism (to name a few issues) has influenced even God's church to morph into something quite different from what it was in its infancy.

Which brings me to the reason why you should read this book: While *Misfit* is written to teens, it will move adults who work with teens, too—in fact, its courageous words will challenge you to critique the core values that drive the kind of ministry you're providing to youth. I believe *Misfit* also will move you to make some tough decisions about realigning your values with practice.

Because if we don't evaluate ourselves and the reason Jesus called us to pour his life into the youth we serve, we'll continue to minister without reflection.

I pray that God will speak to you as you read this book and that his speaking and prompting will lead you to embrace "misfits."

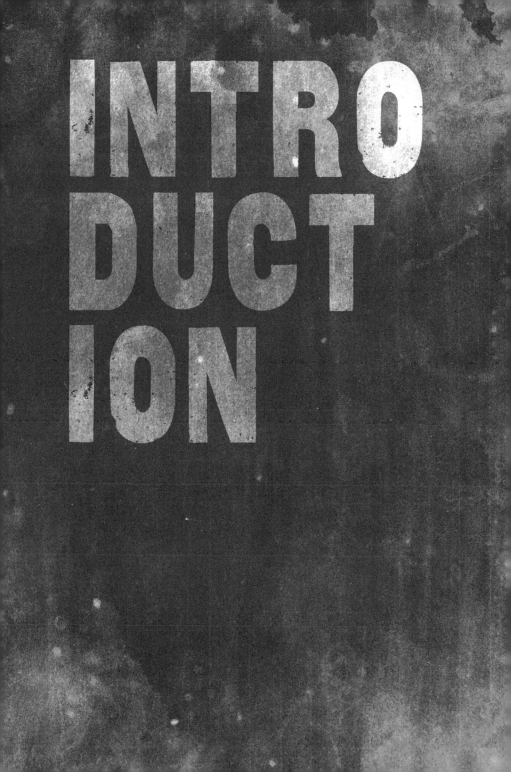

INTRODUCTION

I'M CHRIS DURSO. I'M IN MY

mid-20s and am the pastor of Youth Explosion, a ministry for teens and young people in New York City.

I'm also a misfit.

Since you're reading these words right now, my guess is that you're a misfit, too—or at least believe you might be one.

You are the reason why I wrote this book.

Hundreds of kids come to Youth Explosion every Friday night, and they know all about being misfits—it's a concept we've been exploring together for the last three years or so. And since my students have resonated so well with being misfits, I figured a lot of other teens outside Youth Explosion would want to know about it, too—so this book was born.

I don't know about you, but I struggled for many years to follow God—and I'm a pastor's kid! Plus, my brother was my youth pastor. So God and church and the Bible were around me all the time. I never wanted to hurt my parents, but I wanted to please my friends, too—so I played both sides. I was smoking weed and singing in the youth choir. I was always going back and forth, trying to sabotage my relationship with God so I wouldn't feel worthy to serve in ministry—yet I was scared to live for God. It was only after I started living on my own at college did I decide to follow Christ and put him first in my life.

Since I made that decision, I've reflected on my life and discovered that all the confusion and double-mindedness (we'll get to that concept later in the book) I'd been going through were because I'd been trying so hard to blend into my surrounding culture—instead of standing out as a misfit. I was resisting and fighting the drives and passions God planted in me and gifted me with after I became a believer in him.

But the more I've let my misfit-ness shine through, the more God's been showing how misfits like me can actually change the world. That's been amazingly exciting!

This book takes you on a journey through the process of living your life as a misfit for God. The first chapters help you identify your own misfit characteristics and encourage you to step into the challenges God's called you to contend with. The later chapters deal with bigger issues and struggles you'll encounter on your journey. Since each chapter in the book builds on the chapter before it, I encourage you to read the book in chapter order and not jump around—that way you can think through the processes in a natural way. There are also discussion questions at the end of each chapter; feel free to take your time with them, as they're designed to help you internalize all of the aspects of what it means to live your life as a misfit for God.

May you come away from reading this book feeling empowered and encouraged to reach deep down within yourself and become the leader, the pioneer, the revolutionary—indeed, the misfit—who truly dwells within every Christian walking upon this planet.

CHAPTER 1

FINISHING BEFORE YOU START

WE'RE THE MESSIAH'S MISFITS.

—1 CORINTHIANS 4:9 (*THE MESSAGE*)

LET'S START WITH THE WORD

that sparked your curiosity, the one that grabbed your attention because it's unusual.

It's a rarely used word—and maybe that's because when it's stated, it tends to make everyone uncomfortable.

It's the title of this book.

It stands out because it rarely fits in.

Misfit.

Here's how our culture defines *misfit*: one who's uncomfortable with his or her surroundings and is seen as disturbingly different from others.

Not too positive.

Is that why the word bothers us so much? Why we feel uneasy when someone is labeled a misfit? Even more so, is that why most of us would rather not be labeled as one?

Obviously most everyone wants to fit in. Most people want others to accept them—they even want to meet the standards others set for them. Everyone wants to be appreciated, agreed with, and understood.

But even though we strive so hard for acceptance, I bet we feel rejected more often than accepted. Most likely you've felt like the oddball at one time or another. I'm pretty sure there was a time in your life when you felt as though the word *misfit* was plastered across your face.

Take a second and think about it: Maybe you were the kid who never got picked for the dodgeball game. Maybe you always dressed differently because you hated clothing fads—and you still do. What about the time you showed up to that "Sweet 16" totally underdressed (or overdressed), and the experience wasn't so sweet?

Does it go deeper? Maybe you live in a neighborhood where you're the only one of your ethnicity. Remember that time when you walked into a room and everyone just stared at you like you didn't belong?

Or deeper still? How about that time you felt as though you were the only person who saw the world the way you do? No one understands you—no matter how hard you look or how long you wait. You might live on the same block or sit in the same classroom, but all the others look at you as if you're from another planet.

It's horrible to feel left out—to be rejected because of your likes and dislikes. When people just write you off because you don't act, speak, smell, hear, dress, carry on, look, or think the way they do. Totally misunderstood. An outcast. It's dreadful.

AN ALTERNATE DEFINITION

Sure, not many people want to break the flow and order of things. In fact, most people just "go with the flow" because everyone else does the same thing—it's the path of least resistance. The passive reaction that lets you fly under the radar unnoticed. No controversy. No tension. And no one labels you a . . . *misfit!*

How's that first definition sounding to you now?

Maybe what's really dreadful is believing there's something wrong with *us* if we don't agree with everyone else.

But maybe you're not supposed to act or think like everyone else. Maybe you're meant to be different—to go against the grain.

Let's try an alternate definition of *misfit*: "One who goes against the grain . . . because it's the right thing to do."

If that's what it means to be a *misfit*, I say go for it! And that said, we shouldn't shrink from the first definition, either—as misfits, we should be uncomfortable with our surroundings . . . and we should be disturbingly different from others!

And a big part of being a misfit is living out and expressing your thoughts and feelings, even when they're unpopular.

You can suppress them for only so long. Keeping them bottled up can slowly kill you from the inside out—literally.

Let me tell you a story about a guy nicknamed "U" who started off just like many of us.

EUGENE

I can't remember the first time I met Eugene, but I do remember being in a lot of classes with him. From elementary school through middle school, we sat only a few seats away from each other.

What's funny (in a pretty sad way) is that for all those years we sat so close to each other, we shared only a few conversations. If we did talk, it was to ask something like, "Can I borrow a pen?" or "Can I borrow a sheet of loose leaf?

In fact, I'm not sure Eugene spoke much to anybody. But one of the few things I do remember him saying was that he wanted us to call him "U" instead of Eugene.

I wouldn't go so far as to say he didn't have any friends, but he certainly was the kind of kid who was easy to forget. People didn't have any reason to dislike him because he never bothered anyone. He was a straight-A student and always very polite. If I ever dropped my pencil, "U" would pick it up for me. If anyone were about to walk through the same doorway as "U," he'd hold the door and offer a friendly smile.

Other than that, I couldn't tell you a single thing about him. He was just "U."

A NEW "U"

On the first day of eighth grade, I was anxious to see my friends again. It seems as though summers in New York last a few weeks longer than in other places, and that gave me an opportunity to show off some of my summer clothes. Typical NYC guy-fashion of the '90s: Air Jordan sneakers, basketball jerseys, denim shorts, matching "fitted" baseball cap. (Say what you want—they were cool back then!)

I remember it was particularly hot that first day of school. My friends and I rushed to homeroom hoping the 50-year-old air conditioners were running at full blast. But of course they weren't—in fact they'd broken down a few years before. At least the windows were open! So the humid NYC air circulated through the classroom with the help of industrial fans.

You get the idea. *Hot*.

Then it happened.

An unfamiliar-looking guy stormed into the classroom with a look of disgust on his face. Eyes covered in black eyeliner peeked through long strands of jet-black hair. Despite the heat, his body was covered from head to toe in black clothing. He wore a long trench coat that hung loosely over his T-shirt and wide leg jeans, which were tucked into his knee-high commando boots. And silver chains hung from the belt loops on his pants.

He stomped to a desk at the back of the classroom and furiously slammed down his backpack—*bang!* He made it obvious that he was there but didn't want to be. No one dared look at him.

Later on, while I was pointlessly fanning myself, I caught a second glimpse of the "new kid." And suddenly I realized the "new kid" wasn't new at all.

It was "U"!

As I stared at him in disbelief, he caught me looking at him. We made eye contact. I gave him a head nod and a halfway awkward smile. But "U" just gave me a cold stare—so cold that I had to look away. It was obvious he knew who I was but just didn't care.

Quiet, nice, "regular" Eugene had intentionally changed into dark, angry "U." He no longer went unnoticed. Instead of everyone looking past him, now they stared at him. And talked about him. The formerly least-popular kid in school was now the talk of the hallways.

We were all very aware of his "total body makeover," but it went deeper than that. Now "U" was one of the meanest kids in school, and he hung out with all the rough kids. It made perfect sense, though; he fit in perfectly with them now.

Now "U" was invited to every party—even the ones I wasn't invited to! He had his own table in the cafeteria, and he never had to wait in line. His new look definitely got him the respect and attention he must have been craving.

Then one day I was sitting on a bench in the school office, waiting to meet with my guidance counselor, when in walked "U." He sat down next to me. We didn't say anything for a while. But then someone tripped or something, and all I remember is that we couldn't help but laugh. And for the next 10 minutes, we talked and shared some of our own embarrassing experiences.

Soon I got called into my appointment, so I said, "Later." And I walked away thinking to myself, *Did that really happen?* It was a side of "U" I'd never seen before. He was friendly and warm—without his usual tough exterior.

Then it hit me: *That was the kid I used to sit next to but never really knew because I, like everyone else, had never taken the time to get to know him.* We'd actually pushed "U" to make his drastic conversion.

Sadly, a few days after our encounter in the school office, Eugene was found dead on the floor of his bedroom with a suicide note next to his face.

The note read:

> Dear World,
>
> I'm not well. I'm writing you this letter to apologize for not helping you move forward. I knew inside of me that I was supposed to aid you in something—what that was, I never figured out. On a daily basis, you found a way of amazing me. You had a huge impact on my life. I wish you could say the same about me. I felt like I could relate to you because I saw in you the things I could help change and possibly better.
>
> There was so much I wanted to accomplish in you and for you. I know there were parts of you that needed what was inside of me. I would have loved to help, but I got in my way. I knew I was put here for a reason. Too bad you

never got the chance to really know me. I always wanted to make a difference, but I always felt I was too different. I knew the way I felt about you would somehow set me apart, but I chose to give it all up to fit in. I was born a Misfit; and now that I think about it, that was when I was happiest. That was when I knew there was a greater purpose for my life. I was so concerned with being accepted that I changed who I was. That was when I really died. That's the day I stopped caring about you and became consumed with what mattered to others. Sorry. I could have done something great.

Eugene

Maybe you're thinking, *Poor Eugene—what a sad way to end up.* That's very true. In fact, it's part of the point of this book: I want to make sure you don't end up like Eugene.

He recognized that he was a misfit. That's even the word he uses in his suicide note. But if he'd accepted who he really was, Eugene would probably still be here today.

The point of my sharing my "U" story is to demonstrate how important it is to guard the potential that's inside of you— yes, even those things you believe make you a misfit!

Because the day you give up on your potential is the day you cease to exist.

WHY IT'S GOOD TO BE A MISFIT

There are qualities inside you that are absolutely unique to you. Yes, that does make you different—even a misfit, perhaps—but it's also pretty incredible!

Isn't it awesome to consider the fact that if each of us engaged the world using our own God-given methods, insights, and potential—but without trying to change who we are and conform and feel less like misfits—we'd make history?

I won't lie. This path will be difficult to travel at times. But we're in this together. We're the Messiah's misfits . . . Christ's misfits . . . God's misfits.

Misfits are created to bring change to this world for God's glory. And you can choose either to be a part of this group of world changers or to just sit back and let your God-given purpose decay.

You have the free will to decline or accept this mission. If you decline it, please understand that this mission of misfit-ness is more than just a way of living—*it's the very reason you live!* And, sadly, you wouldn't be the first to say no. In fact, you'd merely be the next person in a very long line of people who've declined being all that God wants them to be.

A "MISFIT" CHALLENGE

Here's my challenge to you:

> *I challenge you to walk through the door of opportunity—a door that many have stood in front of, but very few have walked through. Let me warn you: By walking through this door, you choose to not be influenced or pressured by fads, fashion, music, and especially culture. From this point on, you refuse to define yourself by the color of your skin, what*

people say about you, or where you're from. By walking through this door, you refuse to apologize for who you are and instead choose to embrace what God has created you to be—which is an absolutely unique human being set apart to do God's will in the world. By walking through this door, you choose to live outside the box and never settle for the status quo; you choose to accept your purpose, move the world forward, and cause breakthroughs.

Misfits are strong and focused—but they're dependent on God and dependent on other misfits. You can't contain us or hold us back.

By turning to the next page, you're choosing to accept this challenge. You have walked through the door of opportunity. But if you're not up to it, feel free to put down this book and gracefully bow out. Being a misfit is a huge responsibility. Is it something you feel comfortable being labeled as? Or is it something you wish you could change? Do you feel as though accepting this new, positive definition for "misfit" changes how you feel about being one? Or do you feel as though this new label will change others' perceptions of what a misfit is—and what a misfit is capable of doing in the world? Are you ready to start redefining things today? Take some time to think about these things before you make your decision.

CHAPTER 2

"CHANGE, MISFIT, CHANGE" TOUR

DO NOT CONFORM ANY LONGER TO THE PATTERN OF THIS WORLD, BUT BE TRANSFORMED BY THE RENEWING OF YOUR MIND. THEN YOU WILL BE ABLE TO TEST AND APPROVE WHAT GOD'S WILL IS—HIS GOOD, PLEASING AND PERFECT WILL.

—ROMANS 12:2

WELL, HERE YOU ARE—IN THE

"land of misfits." A world where the unconventional is the standard and the ordinary is just plain weird.

On behalf of misfits everywhere, I congratulate you! It takes a special kind of person to take on this challenge. If you judged this book by its cover and picked it up because of the title, then you're on the right path.

You walked through a door that almost no one else wanted to walk through. You're not afraid of what makes you absolutely unique in this world. You're the round peg in the square hole, the rebel—the misfit.

So now it's time to start a journey to an "out of place" place, a land where the unexpected is not only expected—it's *accepted*.

I'll be your tour guide on this revolutionary journey through the land of misfits. And I can't wait to get started. I have so much to tell you and so little time to do it, as you'll start your own journey very soon.

I want to warn you: What you'll see on this tour will change your perspective on a lot of things. And what you know as "Earth" will look very different once you're done.

It's very important that you don't get too comfortable because we'll find ourselves in some difficult—indeed *uncomfortable*—situations, and we'll deal with some discomforting-yet-revealing emotions.

So pace yourself if you need to, but please make sure you stay with the rest of the group—don't get sidetracked. It's very important that you stay focused.

You'll notice some sights and sounds that others won't. There are things that will bother you that won't bother others—just like what bothers them may not bother you. God created us that way.

Remember: The things you notice and want to change will naturally cause you discomfort—but they're big parts of who you are as a misfit. Their existence will drive you and motivate you and keep you moving forward.

In this world we celebrate leaders, entrepreneurs, and revolutionaries who've acted on their discomfort. It would be foolish of us not to pay tribute to these pioneers of change—for they have much to teach us. Still, our world is in terrible shape because more people like them haven't stepped up.

Unfortunately there haven't been too many of them. I wish I could say we misfits have more forefathers and mothers than we do. But, sadly, we don't.

THE *REAL* REASON YOU'RE HERE

But that's where you come in—the real reason you're here! Because you're absolutely unique, you have passions that have *never been felt* and dreams that have *never been dreamt.* You embody earth-changing resources—resources the world's never seen!

You may not realize it now, but you have the answers to so many of humanity's questions!

Okay, by now you may be saying, "Whoa, whoa! Slow down!" Sorry. Maybe I'm getting ahead of myself. I get really passionate when I'm around people with great potential.

You know what *really* blows my mind? Neither of us honestly knows what you're truly capable of! Not to mention what you might achieve if and when you actualize your potential.

DEEP CHANGE THROUGH DEEP DISCOMFORT

Think about it: We owe all of our advances and achievements to those who believed change was needed—and then *acted* on those beliefs.

From the development of the Internet to the harnessing of nuclear energy and our strides in medicine, mathematics, and the arts, we owe it all to the passions, dreams—and yes, *discomfort*—of those before us.

This elite group of leaders, explorers, and pioneers—*misfits*—isn't very big, though. Because of all the billions upon billions of people who've ever walked the earth (who can even guess how many people have lived since time began!), this group encompasses the smallest of fractions.

Now, that's not to say that only a small group of people are embodied with world-changing potential. Far from it. In fact, all of us have that potential because each one of us is absolutely unique. The difference is that this small group of misfits represents those *who've taken action and made a way for change*.

Try to imagine how far our world would have progressed by now if every human—both today and in the past—put their world-changing resources into effect, turning their potential into actuality.

Take a minute and imagine the possibilities. Don't limit your mind to just science and mathematics. Think about poverty. The arts. Education. Exploration. Civil rights and equality. Let it all sink in.

Don't get me wrong: I understand *why* people choose not to step up, *why* they choose to leave their potential unrealized and their desires unfulfilled. It takes work, dedication, and an almost *insane* amount of determination to take action.

THE KEY FACTOR: JESUS

Let's be clear: For the purposes of this book, all misfits are Christians—but not all Christians are misfits.

So on this tour, this journey, it's important to realize that the whole misfit idea is based on *one choice*: To accept or decline God's plan for your life.

To accept means that if you're a Christian, you can tap into your God-given potential, recognize your absolute uniqueness, and go off and be a misfit world-changer for Jesus.

If you're not a Christian, you can still get in touch with God's plan for your life by starting with the most important relationship of all—with Jesus—and go from there.

And to decline God's will for your life . . .

THE LONG HALL OF CHANGE

There it is, just a few feet to your right: The big, wide entrance to the "Long Hall of Change." Let's take a quick look inside.

You'll notice this hallway is immense. See all the pictures hanging on the wall? Lots of different kinds of people. Misfits come in all shapes, sizes, genders, and colors. While some were successful, others failed. Some made great choices, while others made poor choices.

All in all, our "misfitness" isn't determined by anything other than the decisions we make day to day. And all of these decisions will involve some kind of compromise. That compromise, regardless of intent, has caused you to change either for the best or for the worst.

Since the beginning of time, humans have struggled with whether or not to change.

Change is the "WHY" regarding whether people step up, step back, or step in the wrong direction.

A HISTORY OF CHANGE

Let's take a look at how change has shaped our history—because whether or not we love the idea of change, it's been with us through our best and worst times.

CREATION

Let's start with the creation story. (See it there on the wall?) It's represented in the first picture on your left.

The characters are God, Adam, Eve, a serpent, and "change" (in the form of a piece of fruit).

The setting is a beautiful garden. I'm betting this garden was much more beautiful than we could possibly imagine, filled with incredible wildlife, plants, and fruit . . . that all-important fruit.

The fruit that grew in this garden was undoubtedly delectable—and all of it was Adam and Eve's to eat whenever they felt like it. All except the fruit that grew from one specific tree—the tree of "The Knowledge of Good and Evil." God warned Adam that if he or Eve ate from this tree, the result would be death.

They knew the consequences—yet they still chose to eat the fruit. Oftentimes it's easy to judge Adam and Eve for their failure, but we should really take a step back and look in the mirror—because we might be eating from forbidden trees on a daily basis.

To our benefit, we have the whole creation story as a guide—yet we still sin like Adam and Eve did. And neither of them had such a story to guide them. They made a choice based on their free will and, in turn, changed for the worst.

Let's go deeper: What was the *real* reason Adam and Eve chose to disobey God?

Eve engaged in a conversation with a serpent that asked her, "Did God really say, 'You must not eat from any tree in the garden'?" (Genesis 3:1)

Eve answered correctly: "We may eat fruit from the trees in the garden, but God did say, 'You must not eat fruit from the tree that is in the middle of the garden, and you must not touch it, or you will die" (3:2–3).

The serpent then replied, "You will not certainly die" (3:4).

At that point Eve should have walked away from this catastrophic conversation. And Adam, "who was with her," should have stepped in. Instead, Adam and Eve chose to listen to the created as opposed to the Creator—they did what they wanted to do, not what God wanted them to do.

(And that pattern persists to this day, doesn't it?)

As a result Adam and Eve were banished from the garden. They went from eternal life *on earth* to lives that always ended in death.

They understood the consequences of eating from the tree, so why did they choose to do so?

The answer is they were seduced, and that pushed them

over the edge. Their eyes were dazzled, their taste buds were tempted, and they traded temporary pleasure for what would have been a wise choice with eternal consequences.

God has given us minds and emotions to use freely. But God has also given us Scripture that shows us the outcomes of our good and bad decisions—the consequences. Our lives may not be recorded in the Bible, but our lives operate by the same rules, and we face the same consequences for following (or not following) those rules.

They are always life . . . or death.

ON THE RIGHT SIDE OF THE HALL . . .

As we continue to walk through the Long Hall of Change, you'll notice it's organized in a very specific way: The left side is covered with pictures of those who've made bad decisions, while the right side is full of images of those who've made good decisions.

You'll notice that Jesus pretty much owns the right side of this wall for about 33-and-a-half years.

What? You don't believe that his decision to not give in to temptation counts? It does count! Jesus said no to sin and stood his ground. He stepped away from all temptations. How can you be more out of place (in a very, very good way) than Jesus? He's the ultimate misfit! We have a lot to learn from him—but we'll do that later.

DR. MARTIN LUTHER KING, JR.

Come on, guys. Let's move a little further down the hall. If you look to the right, you'll see a picture of Dr. Martin

Luther King, Jr. I believe we're all pretty familiar with him, but allow me to go through the highlights anyway.

King was (and still is) a human rights icon. He was an American minister, activist, and leader of the African-American civil rights movement, not to mention a recipient of the Nobel Peace Prize and the youngest person to ever receive the award at that time.

Although he gave many rousing speeches, which are often quoted to this day, King was about more than words.

He suffered a great discomfort. (Remember that from earlier in our tour?) In the face of violent and dehumanizing treatment of black people, King dreamed of racial equality and segregation's end. This dream propelled him toward change. Likewise, always allow your dreams to propel you toward change.

King acted on his discomfort. His actions—as well as the actions of countless others who followed his lead with peaceful public demonstrations and resistance to injustice—paved the way for the success of the civil rights movement.

But King's dreams were more than ideas; they were the foreseen outcomes of daily action and mobility toward a goal. He proactively helped cause change, regardless of the cost. Despite constant attempts to stop him, King's will was steadfast.

On April 16, 1963, King wrote "Letter from a Birmingham Jail" from inside one of the city's cells. He'd been arrested in the Alabama city while holding a peaceful protest against the hiring practices of white business owners. The letter was written as a response to the public statements of eight fellow Southern religious leaders who called King's actions "unwise and untimely." (Remember, these were *religious* leaders—not people we'd typically label "racist.")

Check out this excerpt from King's letter:

> My Dear Fellow Clergymen:
>
> While confined here in the Birmingham city jail, I came across your recent statement calling present activities **"unwise and untimely."** Seldom do I pause to answer criticism of my work and ideas. If I sought to answer all the criticisms that cross my desk, my secretaries would have little time for anything other than such correspondence in the course of the day, and I would have no time for constructive work. But since I feel that you are men of genuine good will and that your criticisms are sincerely set forth, I want to try to answer your statements in what I hope will be patient and reasonable terms . . .
>
> But more basically, I am in Birmingham because injustice is here. Just as the prophets of the eighth century B.C. left their villages and carried their "thus saith the Lord" far beyond the boundaries of their home towns, and just as the Apostle Paul left his village of Tarsus and carried the gospel of Jesus Christ to the far corners of the Greco-Roman world, so am I compelled to carry the gospel of freedom beyond my own home town. Like Paul, I must constantly respond to the Macedonian call for aid.

King could have backed off because of what society—and even the church—thought about his beliefs (not to mention the constant death threats again him and his family).

But like all true misfits, King let nothing stand in the way of his dream.

What I love most about his response is that it's direct but loving. Instead of rejecting them, King instructed them. He didn't allow his emotions to dictate his response.

King didn't bury his fellow clergymen with sarcasm or harsh words; instead, he used the letter as a tool to explain his dream to those who didn't share it . . . yet.

Paul writes in Romans 2:4 (*The Message*) that "God is kind, but he's not soft. In kindness he takes us firmly by the hand and leads us into a radical life-change."

Change isn't often brought on by rude, sarcastic, or malicious means; rather it's typically brought on by kindness and love. King applied that principle not only to his response to the clergymen, but also to the way he behaved during marches and demonstrations—all nonviolent.

And because King embraced the life of a misfit and put his dreams into action, the world has been slowly changing ever since.

NEXT STOP

As we move forward on our journey, you'll notice that some people don't understand what you're trying to accomplish. They just can't see what you see. Don't let that rattle you. Make sure your focus stays strong.

Each decision you make, like your purpose, is yours alone to make. Our society will often try to make you do what it wants you to do; our culture doesn't care if what it wants you to do goes directly against your core beliefs as a Christian. So rather than listening to the noise of this world, listen to the One who created it. What are the things in your life/that you see in the world that bring you the deepest discomfort? Do you view these "discomforting" things as too big and too difficult to overcome? If so, do you wish that you could? Are there any discomforts in the world that you find yourself daydreaming about solving? If so, which ones? Do you agree with the idea that the only difference between "average" people and icons like Jesus and MLK is the choices they've made? If so, how does that affect the kinds of choices you want to make now and in the future?

I don't want to cut short our time in the "Long Hall of Change." But we're running behind, and it's time for us to meet up with the others.

CHAPTER 3

ADMITTING IS THE FIRST STEP

EMBRACING WHAT GOD DOES FOR YOU IS THE BEST THING YOU CAN DO FOR HIM. DON'T BECOME SO WELL-ADJUSTED TO YOUR CULTURE THAT YOU FIT INTO IT WITHOUT EVEN THINKING.

—ROMANS 12:1 (*THE MESSAGE*)

HEY, SORRY WE'RE LATE

everyone. We hit a detour at the "Long Hall of Change." Thanks for waiting for us before starting—and for saving us two seats.

As you can see, the chairs are arranged in a circle—and on each chair you'll find a bullhorn. Why a bullhorn? And why are we sitting in a circle? This will probably be one of the lightest moments of our trip. We'll get to help each other let go of the heavy, unnecessary things we've been holding on to for a long time—without even realizing it.

Initially this may feel uncomfortable or strange, but it's important that we lighten our loads—or else we can't continue on our journey. Let's begin!

GETTING TRANSPARENT

You might be tempted to speak softly during this part of the journey. We can all agree that when it comes to sharing our secrets and struggles, we naturally tend to rush past them—barely whispering.

So I want to make sure you listen to yourself as clearly as possible—that's where the bullhorns will come in handy. We must admit out loud, both to ourselves and to each other, what we're dealing with today.

It's also important that we listen to each other and support one another during this process—which is why the chairs are in a circle. The set-up of the chairs will help us realize that we're all on the same level, that no one is superior to anyone else. Plus, they show how we're all connected to each other—connected because we're sharing this common process.

Let's take our seats and begin our time of sharing. Hmm . . . who should start? You all look so interesting. Okay, let's start with me.

Hi, my name is Chris Durso, and I'm a nonrecovering misfit. I'm a misfit because I'm uncomfortable with my surroundings. There are so many things that make me uneasy in this world. But they all pale by comparison with my biggest discomfort: Christians who give Christians a bad name. What bothers me the most is when these Christians preach one thing but practice something else. I don't want to come off holier than thou—because I was that Christian! I preached one thing and did the opposite my entire teenage life.

I wish I had the time to tell you about all the horrible choices I've made. If a lack of wisdom and foolishness were sports, I'd be the Kobe Bryant of each.

My main issue was that I didn't truly follow the examples I appeared to be following. I'd say one thing and then do the opposite. I honestly wanted to do the right thing—but often I didn't.

But even as normal as it was to contradict myself, I felt as though something inside was telling me I was wrong. I always knew when I was wrong, but I still made the same mistakes over and over again.

I'm so grateful that God is big on recycling. God should have thrown me out a long time ago.

I won't tell you my whole life story just yet, but I'll share a snippet of it.

MY "RETREAT"

When I was about 17, I went to a cabin with a couple of my youth leaders. I had no idea why I was on this "retreat." I mean, the guys I was with were so much more developed in their spiritual lives than I was. I wasn't really a Christian; I just pretended to be one. I was nowhere with God.

That didn't really matter to my youth leaders or to my brother Adam, who was the youth pastor at the time. They saw potential in me that I didn't. I had an amazing time at the cabin, and I really felt as though I'd met God that weekend. I left there feeling like I had friends and leaders who cared about my spiritual well-being. That meant a lot to me.

I thought I was changed forever. I really did. I thought I was ready to take on this world, especially with this new support system around me.

I returned home to Queens and then went to Brooklyn around 5 p.m. to hang out; it was a very bright, beautiful Saturday afternoon. And I felt as though I'd been handed a new chance to finally get it right.

THEN ANOTHER KIND OF RETREAT

Next thing I knew, I was sitting on a stoop on Madison Street with one of my best friends. But inside I knew I shouldn't be there. I was wishing I'd made a better choice, but I didn't. We had nothing to do except get high. So we put our money together, and I made my way across the street to a drug dealer who was standing next to a pay phone near a bus stop.

While we were making the transaction, everything in me wanted to jump on a bus and escape. But I didn't—I chose to stay. And as we're swapping the marijuana and the money, the dealer told me something that still blows my mind . . .

Wait! Before I tell you what he said, it's important to reveal that we were standing about five minutes away from the church where my father was the senior pastor, my brother Adam was the youth pastor, and a musical production about my mother's life—*Maria, Maria: The Real West Side Story*— had just completed its run. The musical dealt with how my mother met Christ and was then delivered from abuse, depression, and an intense drug problem. The church put on the production 17 times, and I even acted in it. At each performance there were anywhere from 800 to 1,400 people in attendance . . . and guess who was one of those attendees?

So the drug dealer told me in the most sincere way, "Hey, you know that play they did at your church—the one about your mom? Well, I went to it and really enjoyed myself. Please tell her that it really touched my life."

I knew right then that I'd blown it. I felt like I'd let go of everything God had done for me on that retreat.

But what bothered me the most was that I was a hypocrite. At that moment—and many others like it, many times before—all I could think was, *Why am I here again?*

SABOTAGING GOD'S PURPOSES

Too many times in my life I've had great experiences with God, and then I've made some really terrible, almost self-destructive decisions—choices that, in my mind, cancelled out what God had just accomplished in me. It was as if I were trying to sabotage God's purposes.

But for some reason, God loves using the foolish for his glory. By allowing God to use us despite our shortcomings—and by getting out of our own way—we can accomplish so much more than we could ever realize on our own.

I grew up in my dad's church and my brother Adam's youth ministry (Youth Explosion, which I'm now leading). Adam constantly encouraged us to bring change to this world by reading us Acts 17:6 (NKJV)—"These who have turned the world upside down."

Adam never excluded me, even though I deserved to be. Instead, he prayed for me, loved me, and encouraged me to keep going. When my youth leaders saw I wasn't living out my Christianity, they still encouraged me.

LAY DOWN YOUR BURDENS

Their unwavering support is exactly why I'm now with you on this journey: *I want to encourage you to keep going!* You can get through the difficulties you're facing. But in order to get past them, you have to admit they're there—and that might be the hardest part of letting go of the baggage in our lives.

Proverbs 18:21 says we have the power of life and death in our tongues. So let's start putting that into practice and use both abilities of this powerful body part. Because through our prayers, we can speak life into the dead areas in our souls—and bring death to those things that bring us down.

So let's admit our faults and struggles to God. Doing so will allow us to take the necessary steps to deal with them so we can become who God wants us to become.

Maybe you're struggling with an addiction, low self-esteem, anger, lust, or complacency. Maybe it's something harder— or maybe it's something less serious. Remember: Even the "small things," if left unchecked, can grow into bigger struggles.

It doesn't matter how old you are, where you were born, where you were raised, where you go to school, how much money your family has, or how many friends you have—

struggles find their way into everybody's lives. Therefore, whatever your struggles are, deal with them now so they won't bring you down later. Kill them today so you can live freely tomorrow.

DON'T FOLLOW KING SAUL'S EXAMPLE

In 1 Samuel we learn about King Saul—a monarch who had the chance to be a great king, but because of a few unwise decisions, failed.

Saul became the king of Israel while the nation was at war. The prophet Samuel, who acted as God's mouthpiece, instructed Saul on the way he should lead his people. But despite this divine instruction, Saul made his own decisions—and they were bad ones. His worst one was not killing off the defeated Philistines (1 Samuel 14:46). So these enemies of Israel regrouped, strategized, and attacked again (1 Samuel 17). This time they had a secret weapon—a giant named Goliath. By this point the Israelites were too scared to fight back.

If Saul had just done what God commanded him to do and killed off the Philistine army, there would have been no giant and, more importantly, no more war. But because of Saul's disobedience, the war dragged on. And the Bible says God rejected Saul as king.

In the same way, there are burdens and struggles and issues in our lives that God wants us to deal with and kill off—let's not drag out the battle like King Saul did. A longer war is unnecessary.

And as we knock out the giants in our lives, we're actually enriching the body of Christ. Since we're all interconnected under Christ, my foolish decisions can dishonor our shared faith, just as your wise decisions can honor it and lift it up and advance it.

ALL YOU NEED ARE A FEW WORDS

You can let go of your issues right here, at this very moment, with but a few words—a confession. So I encourage you right now, as you're reading this sentence, to examine your life—the good, the bad, the dark, the ugly, even the shameful—and go through every single item.

(I suggest you take a 10-minute break right here to consider the previous paragraph and how it applies to your life.)

Now for the tough part—the confession. But no worries: Just grab your bullhorn and go for it. Your confession will remove specific burdens from your life—and then you won't need to carry them around any longer. Are there aspects of your life that, if you're honest, consist of "saying one thing and then doing another"? Sometimes it's easier to "sabotage" our spiritual lives before they get started rather than move forward and risk falling on our faces. Have you ever felt this way? Are there people in your life who you look up to spiritually and can help you grow in your faith? If so, have you asked them to help you in this area? If not, why not? Have you ever simply gone to God and asked him to get rid of the things in your life that hold you back from a better relationship with him? Do you believe that God really can work miracles in your life—or, deep down, do you feel it's possible God may not care that much about you? If you feel as though God doesn't care, what's happened in your life to lead you to that conclusion?

NEXT STOP

Oh, look at the time! We must be moving along. As we head to the next part of our tour, I want you to sign in for security reasons. So make your way through that blue door and over to the podium directly to your right. When you get there, you can fill out your nametag.

You have no idea how many frauds have identified themselves as misfits. Still, many people have signed up only to back out later. But we can't do anything about that. Everything here is done according to the honor system.

Make sure you display your nametag where everybody can see it.

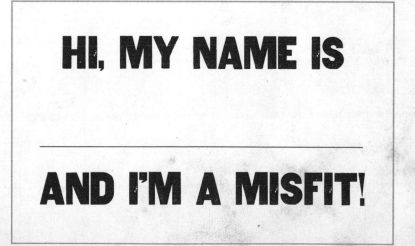

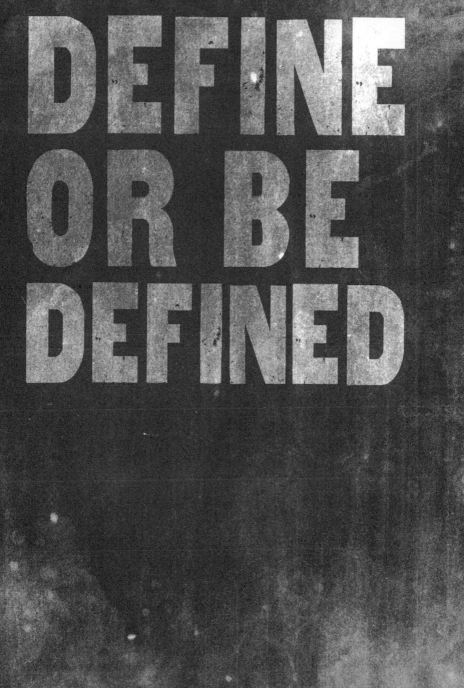

CHAPTER 4

DEFINE OR BE DEFINED

I GAVE THEM YOUR WORD;
THE GODLESS WORLD HATED THEM BECAUSE OF IT,
BECAUSE THEY DIDN'T JOIN THE WORLD'S WAYS,
JUST AS I DIDN'T JOIN THE WORLD'S WAYS.
I'M NOT ASKING THAT YOU TAKE THEM OUT OF
THE WORLD
BUT THAT YOU GUARD THEM FROM THE EVIL ONE.
THEY ARE NO MORE DEFINED BY THE WORLD
THAN I AM DEFINED BY THE WORLD.

—JOHN 17:13–14 (*THE MESSAGE*)

OKAY EVERYONE, MAKE SURE

your nametags are out for all to see. Security might come around and check.

Don't be frazzled by the mayhem in this next room, and don't touch anything either—especially not the piles of paper stacked to the ceiling. And if you see sheets of paper flying through the air, don't worry about trying to grab them—they always land where they're supposed to land. Now let's head inside.

This room is named "Who They Are." It contains the biography of every honorary misfit. See? I told you it's like a madhouse in here; but this is normal for this area.

Let's make our way around the piles of paper and head to the center of the room. I want you to meet the woman responsible for this beautiful mess. Her name is Wiki. She's way too busy to stop and converse with us; but I know that if she could, she would. Watch her work. It's really an incredible sight.

You might be asking yourself what her responsibilities are. Well, let me tell you they're nothing short of mind-boggling. She's writing the biographies of the misfits the world over who are making changes happen. Remember her—Wiki might write *your* biography someday.

WILL THE REAL MISFITS PLEASE STEP UP?

There's plenty of "misfit potential" out there—that's not the problem. No, the problem is that most of us never step up—and step into—our "misfit-ness." We don't believe we're eligible or credible enough for the misfit title when, in fact, we're more than capable of living it out.

See, most people allow others to influence them. They allow others to dictate their value and to define who they are and what they're supposed to do. Me? I believe we should listen to the Creator instead of the created.

We all have definitions that should be attached to our names—God-given definitions. But we have free will, so we often accept only those definitions that other humans have created for us.

Remember what I said earlier about the fact that each person on earth is absolutely unique? That's an inescapable truth.

It follows, then, that God must have made each of us with a specific purpose in mind.

So . . . why do we still look to others to show us who we are to be when God is the only One who knows the truth? And because we don't lean on God for direction, we end up *living lives we were never meant to live.*

Imagine if no one ever lived out his or her purpose. What would our world be like? What would we be like as people? What would drive us to strive for better lives and better futures?

All I know is that a purposeless life is a life wasted. Twentieth-century writer George Eliot put it this way: "I'm proof against the word failure. I've seen behind it. The only failure a man ought to fear is failure of cleaving to the purpose he sees to be best." (*Boys Life*, March 1936)

To know our individual purpose is to know our specific definition, according to God. And when we embrace that definition, we can lead lives of purpose and take action to fulfill those purposes.

A LESSON FROM RUDOLPH

As ridiculous as it might seem, Rudolph the Red-Nosed Reindeer is a great example of this. While not allowing others to define him, he fulfilled his purpose with his specific *red* gifting.

If you're not familiar with the story, here's a quick overview: Santa Claus gets caught in a thick fog while stopped in a small reindeer village on Christmas Eve. The bad weather makes it almost impossible for him to take off again and finish his rounds. But then Santa notices Rudolph's "nose so bright" and asks him to lead and guide his sleigh through the fog. In essence, the physical trait that the other reindeers ridicule Rudolph about and use to make him an outcast becomes the very element that saves Christmas that year.

A corny analogy? Yeah, maybe. But not so fast: Like Rudolph, we're supposed to lead the way in this dark world because as Christians, we have Jesus' light flowing through us.

And like Rudolph, we might get laughed at and ridiculed because of who we are (and who we believe in). But Jesus never called us to "fit in." He calls us to lead the way for others as we follow Jesus. When others realize that we embody the *difference*—the factor that can tip the scales and change the world—they'll want us to lead the way through the danger and uncertainty, too.

DRIFTING FROM GOD (THEN COMING BACK)

I grew up a typical pastor's kid. I attended all church services (and by "all," I mean every single one), and I was accustomed to seeing people get saved, transition into ministry, and be transformed by God. While I was in church, I appeared to be on fire for God. But my friends and I knew it wasn't so.

Picture New York City in the mid-90s. Hip-hop was in its prime and grunge was on the decline. And just like today, the media was down our throats. I was attracted to the alternative lifestyle the media promoted—it was about all the things I naturally wanted. Today I'm ashamed that I bought into that mindset, especially because of how "close" I seemed to be to God—in terms of what people observed of me in church—and how far away from God I truly was.

But soon I tired of living life on a spiritual roller coaster. I had to get off; the ride wasn't turning out to be nearly the adventure I figured it would be. I couldn't deal with all the ups and downs. I needed to live in the reality God had already laid out for me.

So I decided to try living like a true believer—one who stands for change in his community, congregation, and world, and who practices love, compassion, and purity in his life.

I didn't love the *reputation* of the Christians in general, and that kept me away from them for a long time. But I still loved the church.

At the same time, I became uncomfortable with certain activities I'd been practicing while I was drifting away from God. I knew I had to stop taking part.

It wasn't easy. Some people stopped talking to me and acted like they didn't know me. I never wanted to stop being friends with anyone. I knew we didn't agree on certain things anymore, yet I still cared for these people. But for whatever reason, they felt they needed their space from me.

I shouldn't have been surprised. Like 1 Corinthians 4:9–13 (*The Message*) tells us:

> It seems to me that God has put us who bear his Message on stage in a theater in which no one wants to buy a ticket. We're something everyone stands around and stares at, like an accident in the street. We're the

Messiah's misfits. You might be sure of yourselves, but we live in the midst of frailties and uncertainties. You might be well-thought-of by others, but we're mostly kicked around. Much of the time we don't have enough to eat, we wear patched and threadbare clothes, we get doors slammed in our faces, and we pick up odd jobs anywhere we can to eke out a living. When they call us names, we say, "God bless you." When they spread rumors about us, we put in a good word for them. We're treated like garbage, potato peelings from the culture's kitchen. And it's not getting any better.

It's true in my life, and it will be true in yours, too—I'm just warning you. Paul is right when he says it will get rougher and rougher for God's misfits—those who bear Christ's message. I don't say that to scare you, but if I don't speak up now, you might be surprised when you do experience such treatment down the road.

I also want you to know that it's so worth it. In every way.

GETTING LAUGHED AT

Once a relative of mine was hanging out with some friends. For some reason it came up that I was married and had a child. Then as the conversation progressed, one person asked what I did for a living. When my family member replied that I work full time in a church as a youth minister, everyone in the car started laughing. She immediately defended me and told me about the incident later.

That story really messed me up for a few days. What bothered me the most is that these people laughed at me—or at least they laughed at what I do for a living. The Bible tells us that when we're ridiculed like that, we're to count ourselves blessed. But I still had a bit of a pity party over it.

And then one day it hit me: *Of course they'd laugh at what they don't understand.* What gives me a sense of relief is that when their laughter ends and tears start rolling down their cheeks and their hope is gone, I'll be there to love them.

Some people may write us off and define us in terrible ways, but we can't let their definitions dictate who we are and what we can be and do. Let's be who *God* has always wanted us to be. Let's make our words and lives an inspiration for others. So you might want to take some time to think about some of these things: Do you believe you're highly influenced and "molded" by people around you? If so, why? Is it because it's often easier to be passive about your life? Do you feel as though you "blaze your own trail" and ignore people and other forces that would influence you? If so, how did you get to that point? Is there anyone in your life who affects you significantly? Do you feel as though there's a powerful misfit inside you ready to break out . . . but certain fears hold you back? If so, what are they? If you live the life of a misfit for God, do you expect to gain friends or lose friends? One of the circumstances the Bible promises is that Christians will be misunderstood and ridiculed by others. Do you believe this happens because they're being true to their misfit calling? If not, what do you believe is the typical reason?

Now it's time to move forward and look at some even tougher and more uncomfortable issues.

CHAPTER 5

UNCOM FORT ABLE

"NOT ONLY THAT—COUNT YOURSELVES BLESSED EVERY TIME PEOPLE PUT YOU DOWN OR THROW YOU OUT OR SPEAK LIES ABOUT YOU TO DISCREDIT ME. WHAT IT MEANS IS THAT THE TRUTH IS TOO CLOSE FOR COMFORT AND THEY ARE UNCOMFORTABLE."

—MATTHEW 5:11 (*THE MESSAGE*)

AS WE WALK DOWN THIS

new hallway, you'll notice that you soon need to hunch over—and eventually you'll start crawling. Don't worry. You're not shrinking—the hallway is!

That's right. The hallway is gradually getting smaller; and the space is getting tighter, hotter. Soon it will become more difficult to breathe. You'll be quite uncomfortable, to say the least.

We're en route to a place that contains our entire history and will help you understand why this facility was created in the first place.

You know, up 'til now I haven't told you exactly where we are—or, for that matter, where we're headed! You just happened to pick up a book, turn its pages, and all of a sudden you're on a tour with me as your guide.

But a tour of . . . what? Why does this place exist?

We'll get to all of that. But for now, all I can say is that this place exists for you, for us—the misfits. I understand this new journey may be a little scary for you, but I also know that embarking on it is probably one of the best decisions you've ever made.

Personally, this process saved my life. It allowed me to unleash all the potential inside me.

Let me share more of my story with you. Hopefully it will help us pass the time as we crawl.

MY FIRST MEETING WITH "MISFIT"

When I first really thought about the word *misfit*, I became quite uneasy. I was on my way to the bank when I passed a skater. I couldn't help but read his T-shirt. It said MISFIT in bold print.

I'd seen the word before, of course. But on this day it triggered something inside of me. I was genuinely intrigued. I knew at once that this was a "God moment." Although I'd never realized how this word defined me, I'd always unknowingly identified with it.

I can remember many times when I felt like a misfit. In gym class I was the kid who got picked tenth or eleventh—for teams with only 10 or 11 players! I was the "white boy" who loved hip-hop and had to express it in every way possible. Growing up I had ADD, so I was the student who needed "extra help." I remember how my teachers always corrected me—in fact, they couldn't understand how I answered *any* question correctly.

I just understood things in my own way.

I didn't mind *trying* to learn things their way. But when it came to writing, we didn't see eye to eye. My English teachers would say, "Chris, your writing is unique because you write how you think—but that doesn't work." I always thought to myself, *Why not?*

I mean, it's fine that these formats and writing styles are in place, but this is *my* writing style. Isn't writing supposed to be all about self-expression? I loved being unique! But it was a tough process—I always felt like a square peg trying to fit in a round hole. I guess you could say I've always felt like a misfit.

And that's true now more than ever. Except now that I've seen all the amazing things God can do through me when I live out my misfit-ness, I pray that I'll live my life as an original—matchless and unique.

I'm the youth pastor of a great ministry called "Youth Explosion" in New York City. It's definitely my dream job, but every time I speak to non-Christians about what I do for a living, they can't grasp it. In fact, they look at me like I'm crazy. They see how young I am and the way I'm dressed, and they don't understand why I'd dedicate my life to God.

I have no problem explaining why—in fact, I *love* telling them my reasons. In order for people to understand why we live our lives for God, we need to be vocal and expressive about our faith, yet in a manner that isn't excessive or unattractive.

But I still live out my misfit-ness.

WE'RE HERE!

Ah! We're finally here. No matter how many times I make that grueling crawl, I never get used to it.

That small hole in the wall ahead is our entrance. I know it looks impossible to get through, but trust me—you'll fit.

The path to this spot was intentionally designed. "Why?" you ask. We wanted to make sure that those of us who've deemed ourselves misfits can deal with uneasy, discomforting situations. Since your identity as a misfit is based on your honesty, we have to sweat out the authentic from the unauthentic.

If we can't deal with certain uncomfortable situations, then how are we supposed to deal with our misfit-ness? After all, misfits are misfits primarily because they're uncomfortable.

This place was created by a man who saw a need for leadership—for people like you. (He never wanted to receive credit for any of this, so he asked the only two people who know his identity to always conceal it. Since I'm forbidden to say his name, let's just refer to him as "Mr. X.")

Mr. X saw the mayhem in our world and knew that if the right people were encouraged to deal with it—to lead in our churches, communities, and culture at large—the world could drastically change for the better. So he provided a place where we can equip the willing. There are no age, gender, ethnic, or financial requirements to be here—just that whoever walks (or crawls) these hallways must be willing to live out their God-given potential.

TIKKUN OLAM

As a member of the first graduating class, I recall listening to Mr. X talk for hours about an idea in Judaism called *Tikkun olam*. It means "repairing the world" or "perfecting the world."

This expression is used in the Hebrew phrase *mip'nei tikkun ha-olam*, which loosely translated means "to fix for the sake of the world." This phrase indicates that a practice should be followed not because of scriptural law, but because it helps humanity.

Mr. X couldn't understand how Christians and non-Christians alike could be comfortable living in a world where so much is broken. He often said that if our actions caused someone of another culture, background, or religion not only to take notice of this brokenness, but also help bring it to wholeness, then that would be enough for him. He believed that Christians working toward worldwide change would cause observers to see the truth in God.

"THE HARVEST IS RIPE BUT THE WORKERS ARE FEW"

When Jesus made this statement (Matthew 9:37), he was egging on his disciples to not only wear their title of *disciple*, but also display it in their deeds.

In other words, don't just follow Christ around—spread Christ around through your actions. It is by this (our love) that Jesus said others would know we're Christians. Therefore, whoever comes in contact with us would have to know what we believe—and at the same time second-guess what they believe.

REACHING . . . *CHRISTIANS?*

Mr. X also longed to reach those who consider themselves Christians based on cultural or parental ties. He wanted to influence them toward doing justice to their title as *Christians* by truly following Christ as his disciples.

Mr. X's passion resonated with my personal discomfort, and the result is my belief that I exist to help Christians live out their lives as closely tied to Christ as possible. Mr. X's passion is infectious. It causes others to follow you as you follow Christ—which means they're actually following Christ, not you.

The church is more than 2,000 years old, and there are more than two billion professing Christians in the world. But a lot of them carry warped perceptions of God and so many fuzzy understandings of how they should live out their faith. Our beliefs as Christians (Christ's followers) should be *reflected* in our decisions and actions—but oftentimes they aren't. And not only that, but our beliefs should also be backed up by what we do—still, too often they aren't.

That's a big reason why—despite encompassing 30 percent of all humans—we Christians still feel insignificant. We take actions, make decisions, and speak words on a daily basis that contradict our beliefs. And by "beliefs" I don't mean only spiritual things, but beliefs that affect our world.

I can only speak for myself, but I'm not willing to accept the following cultural decisions without a tussle or two:

- No prayer in public schools
- Abortion
- Child prostitution
- Poverty
- School art programs cut
- Unjust social systems
- Unfair immigration laws
- Needless wars

In our world there are so many unsolved problems and unanswered questions—but *we have the answers*. My prayer is that we believers would more frequently find ourselves in "Einstein moments." In other words, when solutions—such as the theory of relativity ($E=mc^2$)—are universally recognized and accepted because of the relevance of the global issues they solve.

GETTING IN TOUCH WITH OUR ISSUES

Depending on how you're wired, there are different issues that probably weigh on your mind and heart all the time. You know the ones I'm talking about—the issues that stick out to you, the ones you daydream about, the problems that make you angry and take away your peace of mind. The issues that, if given the opportunity, you know you'd do everything you could to solve them.

Here are some of mine—do you resonate?

- Child abuse
- Sweatshop labor
- Prostitution
- Human trafficking
- Depression
- Sexual abuse
- Drug addiction
- Gang crime and violence
- Poverty
- Unhealthy perceptions of God

We must understand that if we're uncomfortable with anything about life on earth, then instead of just getting upset or angry or frustrated, we should use our discomfort as a springboard toward change.

If you see something is broken—fix it!

That's the essence of living in your misfit-ness.

God has endowed us with abilities to see the brokenness in our world—although so many look past it (including fellow Christians)—and change it. Take a second and ask yourself why you feel this way in regard to the issue that causes you the most discomfort.

Go ahead and fill in the following blank: *What issue in this world makes you the most uncomfortable?*

_____

I bet your answer is valid. It's also probably different from the answers of those around you. (Don't worry—that's great! You were specifically designed to feel this way. It's part of your makeup. Go after this issue head-on, without hesitation.)

Also take into consideration that tackling any of the issues that weigh on your mind and heart probably won't be the most monetarily or socially rewarding of paths—but it's YOUR path.

Your fellow misfits may take different routes—as they must, if God is fanning out healing and wholeness to as many corners of humanity as possible. But you should travel *yours* and yours alone—without making any apologies whatsoever. And without giving in to the temptation to abandon your path because sometimes it's lonely.

Just know that the people who are crazy enough to believe they can change the world are the ones who do.

All we need to worry about is living the way God designed us to live—as misfits. I mean, we really need to know it, accept it, and display it. We don't have to try look like, act like, or identify with anyone else. Each of us was sewn into human form by the greatest Designer ever.

You are heavenly *haute couture* . . . so wear who you are proudly. Labels out!

> For you created my inmost being; you knit me together in my mother's womb. I praise you because I am fearfully and wonderfully made; your works are wonderful, I know that full well. —David (Psalm 139:13–14)

When you're uncomfortable with something but don't do anything about it, you end up becoming comfortable in your discomfort—and that just leads you nowhere. (Well, it often leads to whining, too—and nobody likes a whiner!) The path of the misfit is never easy—and it's made harder because so few Christians choose that path for themselves. Does that make you want to step out into the unknown all the more? Or does it scare you to think you might be alone out there? By definition, Christians are misfits—it's part of our spiritual DNA. Since that's true, why do you suppose so many Christians spend so much time and energy blending in? Do you spend time blending in? If so, why? Are you comfortable with the idea that misfits should concentrate on bettering a variety of areas in life that bring them discomfort? Or do you believe that there are only a handful of essential areas that a lot more misfits should spend their time on? Do you believe that being a misfit could also mean being … . beautiful? If so, in whose eyes? Does it encourage you that you're indeed a unique piece of heavenly artwork?

CHAPTER 6

JESUS = MISFIT

ANOTHER FOLLOWER SAID, "MASTER, EXCUSE ME FOR A COUPLE OF DAYS, PLEASE. I HAVE MY FATHER'S FUNERAL TO TAKE CARE OF." JESUS REFUSED. "FIRST THINGS FIRST. YOUR BUSINESS IS LIFE, NOT DEATH. FOLLOW ME. PURSUE LIFE."

—MATTHEW 8:21-22 (*THE MESSAGE*)

ALL RIGHT, IT'S TIME TO

take a break before we continue the tour. How about we make our way to the lounge and get a snack? Today's special is loaves and fishes. (I know, I know—I can't wait either!)

I know we need to get where we're going, but it's okay to take a break. Now we get to eat the meal of choice of Jesus—the head of the misfits.

Yes, I'm saying Jesus Christ was—and still is—a misfit! (We briefly covered this earlier, but it bears repeating.)

No, it's not at all sacrilegious to call Jesus a misfit. Yes, we're talking about the same Jesus. No, you needn't worry. By agreeing with me, you haven't broken any commandments. And yes, you're still saved.

JESUS—THE ULTIMATE MISFIT

Can you think of a better example of someone who was uncomfortable with what he observed on earth—who felt *just a bit* out of place—and then did something about it?

When it comes to fixing what's broken, no one's even in the same *universe* as Jesus.

The thing is, the Son of God didn't *have* to do any of the things he did. He left heaven freely, ministered on earth freely, and died for us freely. Why? He loves us that much.

Jesus didn't use his title or status or power to ease any of his own discomfort either—and, again, he could have. And he didn't build up a wall of resentment or annoyance because of the discomfort he experienced, as we often do.

Think about it: Jesus easily could have ignored us—or worse, killed us and started over. But he knew we needed help, direction, and an example. Even though he's the King of Kings, Jesus became the most humble of servants—he lived and died to serve us. Know anyone even remotely like him?

What else about Jesus makes him a misfit? Just about everything! Consider how he entered this world (conceived by the Holy Spirit), his birth (in a stable surrounded by smelly animals), his station in life (dirt poor with no place to lay his head), and his parents' relationship (their engagement was probably scandalous due to Mary's premarital pregnancy).

That last one's the kicker: Imagine being pregnant before marriage in *those times!* It was very much frowned upon in Jewish culture. Imagine what people said about Mary and

Joseph. (Probably the same things we say about people who get pregnant out of wedlock today.) In fact, had Joseph not taken Mary as his wife, she very well could have been stoned to death.

In the face of all of these forces at work, clearly there was a difference between this pregnancy and all others—ever—since the beginning of time: The *Son of God* was growing in a human womb! *Uh, do ya think the Powers That Be could have orchestrated this one with a just few more problems?*

JESUS—OUR ULTIMATE EXAMPLE

But besides the truth that God had wisdom (beyond our understanding) for why he unfolded Jesus' life the way it unfolded, Jesus is proof that the greatest people can come from the most difficult situations.

Rough backgrounds, strained households, and difficult upbringings don't necessarily mean failed futures. We aren't required to become products of our environments. As a matter of fact, as Christians we're empowered to positively shape the direction of our environments—but they have no power to shape us!

We humans have always struggled with this idea. While some people admit their discomfort with what they observe in their world, rise above the obstacles, and make a difference; the vast majority do nothing. They remain unaware or unconvinced that they can lead others and bring about change regardless of their situations.

MORE MISFITS NEEDED!

Which brings us to another job of misfits—making our lives an example to others. We must demonstrate the potential within all of us to meet the great needs of the world. And we should offer such direction to all with whom we come in contact. Paul states in 1 Corinthians 11:1, "Follow my example, as I follow the example of Christ." Others should be able to look at your life and be positively affected by it in some capacity. My hope is to leave an imprint for Christ on anyone with whom I cross paths.

Think of a plaid pattern—a design of intersecting lines. In essence all of our lives are like plaid: There's a purpose for our paths crossing one another. Therefore, let's make sure those "life intersections" weren't planned in vain.

Like Jesus noted to his disciples at the end of Matthew 9, the work of saving souls requires the participation of many people—many who haven't signed on yet. Jesus calls for more workers not because the task has become too much for him, but because he wants to include us in the joy of ministry.

Here's the end of Matthew 9 so you can see what I'm talking about—

> Then Jesus made a circuit of all the towns and villages. He taught in their meeting places, reported kingdom news, and healed their diseased bodies, healed their bruised and hurt lives. When he looked out over the crowds, his heart broke. So confused and aimless they were, like sheep with no shepherd. "What a huge harvest!" he said to his disciples. "How few workers! On your

knees and pray for harvest hands!" (Matthew 9:35–38 *The Message*)

As was usually the case with almost everything he said and did, Jesus was teaching the disciples (and us) a few lessons. First, he wanted to teach them how to *ask*, as opposed to just waiting for "harvest hands" or helpers to appear. Second, Jesus was trying to help them understand that they needed to take an active role in his ministry.

It reminds me of when parents give their children the chore of cleaning their rooms. Even though parents can probably do a better job of cleaning than their kids, it's about teaching little kids to take ownership of their rooms—and, by extension, understand the concept of responsibility.

Jesus could definitely do a better job of sharing the good news than his disciples ever could. But he understood that part of God's plan for salvation was that humans would take an active role in spreading the gospel.

Jesus goes on to tell his disciples that the human race is "like sheep with no shepherd"—in other words, they need guidance and leadership. Therefore the disciples were not only to follow Jesus, but also lead others by example. This same teaching applies today. We're to live lives worth following— and by doing so, we'll be sacrificing our lives unto, and living our lives for, God.

FLIPPING OUT

Jesus had no problem speaking the truth and standing by his point. Remember the buyers and sellers in the temple?

Jesus took one look at what they were doing, walked over to them, flipped over their tables, and ran them out. Now, since our ability to tell the difference between sinful anger and righteous anger isn't quite at Jesus' level, we probably shouldn't make a habit of flipping over tables and desks in our churches whenever we spot unrighteousness.

However, the impact of the change we're bringing about through our misfit-ness should be figuratively "flipping over" our churches and communities. Will we encounter opposition? You bet we will. Will we be misunderstood? Absolutely. The status quo can be a tough enemy to battle. However, we need to be resistant—yet not stubborn; we need to be secure—yet not prideful; we need to be strong-willed—yet not argumentative.

Remember that infamous statement that kids use on their parents during a dispute? "All the other kids are doing it!" And do you remember the infamous parental reply? "If all of your friends jumped off a bridge, would you do it, too?" Well, the parents are right—and you know it!

In the same way, if something is wrong, harmful, or con-tradictory to our beliefs—whether it's in the church or in the world—then we don't do it *regardless* of who's doing it. And just because something has been done a certain way for really a long time doesn't mean that's the best way to do it, either. Maybe that's just the way people have gotten used to doing it.

Therefore, we need to know *why* and *how* before we *agree* and *do likewise*. And if we end up not agreeing, then we'll shine a big light on the wrong we're seeing so others can see it, too.

JESUS' UPSIDE-DOWN KINGDOM

One of the main factors that makes Jesus a misfit is that he founded a kingdom that's completely contrary to all others on earth—a kingdom where the first is last, where the greatest is least, and where a king exists to serve instead of being served.

Jesus proclaimed that he was a king—yet he loved to converse with sinners. (And not just chatting with your run-of-the-mill sinners in a cafe either. We're talking eating full-on meals with prostitutes and tax collectors—more or less an instant recipe for scandal in first-century Jewish culture.)

Jesus left a throne empty in heaven in order to sleep in the wild. Jesus lived a sinless life, yet chose a criminal's arrest and beating, an unjust trial, public condemnation, and a humiliating and excruciatingly painful execution.

Yes, he allowed the very people he was dying for to kill him. The Son of God crucified by his own creation.

LAYING DOWN OUR LIVES LIKE JESUS DID

"Greater love has no one than this: to lay down one's life for one's friends" (John 15:13). In order for us to lay down our lives for others, we must first die to our own wants and desires. How else could we sacrifice wealth and status to fight third-world poverty or teach the Word of God to those who may forget it once they leave the four walls of the church?

It's all about sacrifice. Sacrificing your time to meet the needs of others. Notice I said "time" and not "life" because in giving our time, we're actually living out the lives we were meant to live out. But sacrificing or giving up our lives—in other words, wasting them—would be doing anything other than what we're meant to do. I think we can all agree that in the past we've all "sacrificed" enough of our lives.

Don't worry if you haven't yet sacrificed for the sake of others. With God, it's never too late to make a change.

Who knows? You may be further along in doing what God has called you to do than you realize. Do you have any interests, talents, and gifts? Regardless of what they are, God placed those gifts and interests inside you for a reason.

The next step is to start using your talents and gifts toward building the kingdom of God.

This is so important to keep in the center of your daily motivations: When we choose *not to* use our talents and gifts for God's purposes, we deny the body of Christ a necessary step forward. That's how essential you are to others—and to God!

So, misfit, get out there and watch what God can do through you. Be about our Father's business just as Jesus was. Once you know your trade, it's time to join God's workforce. In God we can accomplish greatness. Your gifts and talents are the tools God wants you to use to draw others to Christ.

Don't forget: "The harvest is plentiful but the workers are few" (Matthew 9:37).

There's plenty of kingdom work out there; plenty of open positions.

But still there aren't nearly enough workers willing to do the job.

WHY YOU'RE PERFECT FOR THE JOB

The disciples are a great example of what God does for (and through) those who answer this calling.

They were a group of badly flawed, mismatched individuals who differed in social status and background—and they were notoriously slow to understand Jesus. All they shared in common was that they answered the call to follow Jesus.

For that day and time, they were misfits indeed.

But it was this common denominator that allowed the disciples to work together successfully, as their mission would have otherwise failed.

And that's all you need, too.

Jesus uses who he wants, when he wants, and how he wants—regardless of one's race, gender, background, or status. Jesus uses people of all types to reach groups of all kinds. Is there a better way to get the job done? Do you more often identify with Jesus as a misfit like yourself . . . or do you see him as an older brother-kind-of-guy who's better at everything? Somewhere in between? In your opinion, what episode from the Gospels was the defining moment for Jesus as a misfit? Do you feel as though you should be emulating exactly what Jesus did in his life on earth in order to walk his path correctly? If so, what examples come to mind? If not, do you believe there's any episode from Jesus life that we should copy exactly? Now that you've looked at the life of Jesus as a misfit and see all that he's expected from his followers, how will you spend your days differently?

Each one of us—like each of the disciples—has a specific role to play that's crucial to the success of the team. We're all gifted differently to work the field differently.

Let's get to work!

But first—hurry up and finish your meal. We have to get to the media room in about five minutes. We're watching a film about evolution.

And just so you know, we wanted to serve popcorn during the movie. But we're short-staffed, so no one's available to work the machine.

CHAPTER 7

EVOLVE, MISFIT, EVOLVE

WHEN I WAS A CHILD, I TALKED LIKE A CHILD, I
THOUGHT LIKE A CHILD, I REASONED LIKE A CHILD.
WHEN I BECAME A MAN, I PUT CHILDISH WAYS
BEHIND ME.

—I CORINTHIANS 13:11

OKAY PEOPLE, AS YOU ENTER

the media room, fill up the seats at the front first. There shouldn't be any empty chairs.

And make sure you sit next to someone you *don't know*. Take out a pen and pad for note taking. As you do that, I'll set up the projector and make sure the reel is in place. Please, no talking, note passing, or spitwads. Thank you.

3 -   2 -   1

Film flashes on the screen as a narrator's voice begins speaking.

EVOLVE:
TO UNDERGO DEVELOPMENT

For the most part, when we hear the words *evolve* or *evolution*, we most likely think about monkeys turning into humans or the Big Bang.

But forget for a moment all the scientific theories you may have heard in school. For our purposes we'll be focusing on the dictionary definition of *evolution*, which is "to undergo development."

In that sense, humans have always evolved in one way or another.

Imagine if nothing *ever* developed. What would life be like?

1. According to Darwin, we'd all be monkeys.
2. Caterpillars would never turn into butterflies.
3. We'd all be cave dwellers shivering in the cold while a couple of rocks sat in the same spot, day after day, never getting struck together to make a spark for fire.

Now imagine if we evolved . . . but only so far:

1. Had we progressed only as far as the 1800s, we'd still be traveling by horse and buggy.
2. Had we stopped during the 1970s, we'd still be sporting afros, thick moustaches, and bellbottoms, and dancing to disco music.
3. Imagine we stopped during the 1980s: We'd still be using the Commodore 64 . . . and *no Starbucks*! That would be a very rough world indeed.
4. Or what if we'd made it only as far as the 1990s? Some would be wearing baggy clothes all the time and listening to gangster rap, while others would be dreaming about Seattle-based grunge bands. *Oh, you still do that? Nevermind . . . (Heh heh, get it?)*

Without evolution the human race would be stuck in place—no momentum moving it forward.

So that kind of evolution is important.

Now the scientific theory of evolution is based on the idea that organisms change very, very slowly over time in order to cope with and adapt to the changes in their environment.

I can really relate to this idea on a symbolic level, especially as a misfit. In evolution organisms that evolve become stronger than those that don't evolve, and then the weaker organisms eventually die off.

In the same way, misfits can be effective only if we evolve or develop. We do that by recognizing and trying to change what makes us uncomfortable. If we don't, then we become (sadly) comfortable with what makes us uncomfortable. We lose our passion to bring about change, and we eventually cease to exist as misfits. We just blend into the background scenery.

The Bible has something to say about that:

> Do not be conformed to this world (this age), [fashioned after and adapted to its external, superficial customs], but be transformed (changed) by the [entire] renewal of your mind [by its new ideals and its new attitude], so that you may prove [for yourselves] what is the good and acceptable and perfect will of God, even the thing which is good and acceptable and perfect [in His sight for you]." —Romans 12:2 (Amplified Bible)

When we resist our evolution as misfits—when we conform to the world's ways and avoid the transforming of our minds—we lose our misfit-ness. When we like the way things are, when we prefer predictable outcomes, we lose our misfit-ness.

And every now and then, we'd rather go *backward*.

I see it like this: After we're potty trained, we don't go back to wearing diapers. If we did, well . . . let's not even think about what that kind of world would be like! But that was the exact mindset of the Israelites during one part of the Old Testament.

GRUMBLING AND COMPLAINING

The Israelites were divided into 12 tribes that traveled together. They wanted change, and they got it. But after they got it, they tried to go back to the wretched life they'd escaped. Here's a quick synopsis from Exodus:

God sent Moses to the Israelites to rescue them from slavery in Egypt. God delivered them, even parting the Red Sea to enable their escape. The Israelites rejoiced. They sang a song to honor God. God told them to follow Moses so he could lead them to the Promised Land—an amazing land flowing with milk and honey (in other words, paradise).

A couple of days later, they started to grumble and complain—they were thirsty, after all. So God provided water. They complained again because they were hungry: "If only we had died in Egypt." So God dropped bread (*manna*) from the sky. They got quail, too. But they still complained. They were no longer slaves, but they longed for Egypt.

Later some of the Israelite men went ahead to the Promised Land to scout it out. When they saw that giants were roaming the land, they got scared and told the rest of the Israelites what they saw. So what did the people do? Only what they do best—they complained! God got so fed up that he killed everyone who was saved from Egypt and all men 20 years old and older, except for Caleb and Joshua.

The Israelites continually forgot who God was and God's promises to them. In doing so they couldn't evolve spiritually, preventing themselves from entering into all that God had for them. They remained slaves, in a sense, to their selfish, childish attitudes and old ways of living. This led to their dying as old, immature, and complaining adults.

But misfit, don't be too quick to judge the Israelites. Our futures can easily become just as dreadful.

What are some of the childish ways you've brought with you on this journey? What do you need to work on? Your temper? Whining? Laziness? Negativity? Immaturity? Arrogance? Stubbornness? Fear?

Whatever your childish way may be, ask God to help you move past it—and then *move past it*. Be intentional about following God's guidance and lean not on your own understanding.

And every once in a while, look back and realize how far we've all come. Be grateful for your opportunities to learn from others' mistakes and successes. Be grateful, too, for all those who've pushed us forward. (It was a struggle for many to evolve. So when I say they pushed, they *pushed*!) Finally, let's be grateful for our history and always remember it.

FILM STOPS – LIGHTS COME ON – CHRIS ENTERS

Before continuing on our journey, I'm going to have you take an important survey:

1. Are there areas of your spiritual life in need of "evolution"? If so, which ones?
2. The Bible talks about healthy seed thriving and unhealthy seed dying off, as well as healthy branches thriving and unhealthy branches getting discarded. Do you think this is God's version of "survival of the fittest"? Why or why not?
3. How does it make you feel to know that God is highly interested in misfits who simply do what he wants them to do and rely on his strength to do it? Does that sound harder or easier to do than doing life on your own and by your own rules?
4. What "childish ways" do you need to kill in your life in order that you live the misfit life to the fullest and welcome continual evolution in your soul?
5. Have you ever reached a point in your spiritual life when you were "comfortable being uncomfortable"? If so, when did that happen—and why?

Okay everyone, up, up, up! Let's go, go, go! We don't want to keep the doctors waiting. Place your surveys by your seat, and I'll collect them.

It's time for our psychological competence session. So we need to make our way to "The Room of Couches."

As you exit the theater, you'll notice a wastebasket on your left. Please deposit all of your childish ways into this receptacle as you evolve forward.

Thank you.

CHAPTER 8

MISFIT VERSUS MISFIT

BUT WHEN HE ASKS, HE MUST BELIEVE AND NOT DOUBT, BECAUSE HE WHO DOUBTS IS LIKE A WAVE OF THE SEA, BLOWN AND TOSSED BY THE WIND.

—JAMES 1:6

WE'RE ENTERING "THE ROOM

of Couches." Notice the different colored couches spread throughout the dimly lit room? We're now in the most comfortable room in the building—and we're about to experience the most uncomfortable part of the tour. Please pick your couch and lie down immediately.

Try to relax and be at ease.

Close your eyes.

Now listen.

Up to this point, you've seen a lot and received lots of insightful and empowering information. I understand this isn't the simplest stuff to digest. After all, you're not downing soft drinks; this is a *big meal*.

It's not easy to adjust your mindset, especially when life is so difficult. But that's what brings us here. In order to move forward, we have to deal with something that will definitely try to hold you back.

Actually it's not a "thing" at all—it's a person. Someone quite familiar with who you are. This person knows a lot about you—the good and the bad. This person even knows all your secrets. Why? Because this person is always around you. You eat together, bathe together, learn together—even sleep together. Surprised? Embarrassed? Don't be.

I'm talking about . . . *you*.

I'VE SEEN THE ENEMY, AND IT IS US

Some people may get on your nerves and say and do things that physically and mentally hamper you. But no one can hurt you the way *you* can!

More often than not, you're at war with yourself. Spiritually speaking, there's a part of you that knows God has a plan for your life, while another part doesn't believe that at all.

So, *you* are the most critical and negative factor in your journey. Your dark, negative voice will constantly tell you, *This isn't for you!* It might even say, *You aren't good enough to lead others*.

And believe it or not, you may *want* to hear these words because they provide a detour away from your opportunity to lead change, to step into and live out your misfit-ness. Listening to them might allow you to live a "normal" life. You could live life as you please. You won't have to worry about anyone or anything other than yourself. Life would be less strenuous without the idea that you need to embrace your misfit-ness and solve the issues of the world. Who needs that pressure, right? It's so much more enticing to think about living an easy, painless, uncomplicated life. If others don't care, then why should you, right?

Well, no—that's exactly it.

If everyone reacted that way and did nothing, we'd all quickly lose our world-changing potential.

The truth is that there's no such thing as a "normal life." No one lives one—everything's abnormal from the get-go.

And by not accepting what we've been created to accomplish, we'll never feel fully satisfied with what we *do* accomplish in life.

ACCEPTING GOD'S PLAN—*COMPLETELY*

See, by accepting and carrying out God's plan for our lives, we guarantee our success. But when we *partially* accept God's plan for our lives (forget outright ignoring it), we're guaranteed to fail.

Imagine going into a military operation after partially listening to intelligence or while partially carrying out orders. It's a recipe for failure.

Imagine if Joshua only partially listened to God's command or allowed his own doubt to prevent him from doing what God asked him to do. If you're not familiar with the story of Joshua and the great wall, let me share it with you briefly.

God commanded Joshua to walk around the wall surrounding the city of Jericho. God gave Joshua very specific instructions promising that if he followed the directions, the walls of Jericho would come crashing down. God's instructions were for Joshua and all of the Israelites to walk around the wall once a day for six days, and then circle it seven times on the seventh day. (See Joshua 6.)

So what did Joshua do? Exactly what God told him to do. And because he did, Joshua got the very results God promised him. On the seventh day, after the seventh walk around the wall was complete, the walls of the city came tumbling down.

That was simple, right? Yes. Exactly. It was as simple as accepting God's instructions and executing them.

But just because the instructions were simple didn't necessarily make them easy to carry out. Let's think about the possibilities for a moment.

We don't know if the walls started to fall apart slowly as they continued to walk around the wall. How mentally exhausting do you believe this process was for Joshua? Personally, by the fourth or fifth time around on that seventh day of marching, I'd hope to see some bricks popping out or even some dust trickling down the side of the wall. By the end of the sixth lap, at hearing no big rumbles, I would have been full of doubt. I would have been beating myself up and asking, *How dumb could I be to believe that God actually told me to walk around this city seven times today so those walls would fall down?*

But that was never the case for Joshua—he did what he was told, and God gave Joshua what was promised.

Don't get me wrong—I believe it's very possible that Joshua and the Israelites went through some mental battles and fought with their doubts. I mean, these were the same Israelites who had issues about following Moses and believing God for the Promised Land.

But God will never set us up to fail. In fact, by allowing doubt to enter in, *we're* the ones who set ourselves up to fail.

DON'T BE DOUBLE-MINDED

James 1:5–8 says—

> If any of you lacks wisdom, you should ask God, who gives generously to all without finding fault, and it will be given to you. But when you ask, you must believe and not doubt, because the one who doubts is like a wave of the sea, blown and tossed by the wind. Those who doubt should not think they will receive anything from the Lord; they are double-minded and unstable in all they do.

Whenever I think about the term *double-minded*, I instantly recall the story *Dr. Jekyll and Mr. Hyde*. Here you have a very intelligent doctor who creates a powerful and destructive potion that turns him into a completely different person—Mr. Hyde. Soon Mr. Hyde takes over Jekyll's body and mind. Jekyll's friend, Mr. Utterson, tries to help Jekyll, but the doctor—feeling guilty and ashamed—lies to conceal the issue.

Jekyll's potion was intended to separate a person's personality into two—an evil one and a good one. Unfortunately, the potion began taking over and caused Jekyll to randomly change from Jekyll to Hyde and back again. Soon enough Jekyll realizes his research was a mistake, and he takes his own life. In his suicide note, Jekyll writes that if he'd turned into Hyde one more time, there would have been no turning back.

We're often like Dr. Jekyll in that we make bad decisions with good intentions that often result in failure. Sadly these failures are a result of not seeking God's counsel. We rely too much on our own understanding. We create "potions" that change our paths and slowly lead us astray.

Romans 12:3 tells us, "Do not think of yourself more highly than you ought, but rather think of yourself with sober judgment, in accordance with the faith God has distributed to each of you."

And of course we know what Scripture (and English literature) has to say about the problems of double-mindedness. In order for us to steer clear of it, we need direction and clarity of mind, which only God can provide. We can't afford to become intoxicated with our potions. Our work is too important to take risks with our decision making, which—because of our misplaced trust in who we are and an unfortunate lack of trust in who God is—often ends in failure.

Jekyll's will had no say as to when Hyde took over the body. Therefore, Jekyll did things he never would have done apart from Hyde's influence. He even committed murder. Jekyll lost control.

PAUL'S STRUGGLE

In some ways this story is similar to Paul's struggle recorded in Romans 7:15–16.

> What I don't understand about myself is that I decide one way, but then I act another, doing things I absolutely despise. So if I can't be trusted to figure out what is best for myself and then do it, it becomes obvious that God's command is necessary. (*The Message*)

When we first meet Paul in Acts 7, his name isn't even Paul—it's Saul. And that's not the only thing that's different about the man.

Saul was a Pharisee who hated Christians and persecuted them—he even had them killed. The book of Acts records that Paul attended and approved the stoning of Stephen, an early, fervent, Spirit-filled disciple of Jesus (Acts 8:1).

One day, while en route to another persecution, Jesus stopped Saul on the road and spoke directly to him. Here's the account from Acts 9:1-12.

> Meanwhile, Saul was still breathing out murderous threats against the Lord's disciples. He went to the high priest and asked him for letters to the synagogues in Damascus, so that if he found any there who belonged to the Way, whether men or women, he might take them as prisoners to Jerusalem. As he neared Damascus on his journey, suddenly a light from heaven flashed around him. He fell to the ground and heard a voice say to him, "Saul, Saul, why do you persecute me?"
>   "Who are you, Lord?" Saul asked.

"I am Jesus, whom you are persecuting," he replied. "Now get up and go into the city, and you will be told what you must do."

The men traveling with Saul stood there speechless; they heard the sound but did not see anyone. Saul got up from the ground, but when he opened his eyes he could see nothing. So they led him by the hand into Damascus. For three days he was blind, and did not eat or drink anything.

In Damascus there was a disciple named Ananias. The Lord called to him in a vision, "Ananias!"

"Yes, Lord," he answered.

The Lord told him, "Go to the house of Judas on Straight Street and ask for a man from Tarsus named Saul, for he is praying. In a vision he has seen a man named Ananias come and place his hands on him to restore his sight."

Knowing what Saul had been up to in other regions, Ananias was naturally apprehensive. But he obeyed and visited Paul—I mean, Saul—and prayed for him. God then restored Saul's sight.

After his transformation, Saul so despised who he'd once been that he changed his name to Paul. Later in his life, Paul wrote the verse we read earlier—*"What I don't understand about myself is that I decide one way, but then I act another, doing things I absolutely despise."* Thus, Paul allows us to see that he was still pushing back and fighting against Saul.

When we look at it from this perspective, we can really understand why Paul so often wrote about daily death and being a living sacrifice to God.

And just as Paul did, we must daily put to death the bad areas in our lives *before* they take over—something Jekyll lacked the strength to do.

ANANIAS: OBEDIENCE DESPITE DOUBT

Let's focus on Ananias to wrap things up. His obedience and resolve to serve God was exemplary, yet he became just as scared and timid as any of us would likely become if God asked us to perform a difficult task or fulfill a crucial role. He said,

> "Lord, I have heard many reports about this man and all the harm he has done to your people in Jerusalem. And he has come here with authority from the chief priests to arrest all who call on your name."

God responded,

> "Go! This man is my chosen instrument to proclaim my name to the Gentiles and their kings and to the people of Israel. I will show him how much he must suffer for my name."

Even in his doubt and fear, Ananias still obeyed—a difficult and often daunting task for many of us. On this journey you'll often face moments of fear, self-doubt, and timidity. These feelings are normal and to be expected.

What's important is that we, like Ananias, still obey the voice of God and his commands in spite of our doubts and fears. So I want to encourage you to be strong and courageous; fear and doubt are just parts of the process.

There's a part of me that really believes God enjoys and has a purpose behind using us *during our moments of fear*. I believe it allows us to trust God a little bit more and realize more fully that God is in control.

TRUST GOD, THEN GO!

Regardless of whether or not you can relate to Paul, Saul, or Ananias, you are God's instrument. Even though you may be in a dark and ugly state of mind, God can change that. God can and will renew you. Because of your insecurities and fears, you may not understand why or even how God wants to use you. But ultimately the only response to God's call is to GO!

Take a moment and declare to yourself and to God that even though your heart pounds, your palms sweat, and your knees knock, you will go.

The difference between most people and Christ's misfits is that we misfits choose to die to ourselves on a daily basis. We fight our fears, insecurities, doubts, and even Mr. Hydes—and we do it over and over again. Have you heard the saying, "I've seen the enemy, and it is us"? Do you find that's true in your life—that you're often your own worst enemy? If so, in what specific ways is this true? Have you ever felt led by God to carry out a task or mission—but didn't react in complete obedience? (In other words, maybe you obeyed most of what God called you to do, but then you called the shots on a few matters.) How did that work out for you? What have been your biggest triumphs when it comes to hearing and following through with God's will? Reflect on everything that happened, from beginning to end. What have been your biggest struggles in this area? What, if any, circumstances were different between your triumphs and your struggles? The Bible says that Paul had major struggles with doing things that, in his heart, he didn't want to do—and not doing things he knew he should have been doing. Does it encourage you or discourage you that Paul—one of the biggest misfits ever and a powerhouse of the early church—struggled in this way? The account of Ananias is cool not just because he trusted God, but also because he wasn't afraid to voice his doubt to God at the same time—and in the end he obeyed God. Do you think it's a good thing to feel the freedom to voice doubt to God—or do you feel as though there shouldn't be any doubt? (Especially if God is speaking directly to you!)

Take a minute and ask God to equip your mind with the wisdom and mental endurance you need for this journey.

I want to applaud you for making it this far. You seem to be doing well. In the past I've seen grown-ups run out of this room in fear because they allowed their thoughts to get the best of them and their commitment to God to get away from them. Remember, as you allow God to lead, don't allow yourself to get in the way.

Oh man, our time is up! Okay, get up slowly from your couch and let's gather our things. We really have to get going.

Maybe you're wondering where we're about to go next. I can't say just yet, but it's going to be pretty wild!

CHAPTER 9

MISFITS GO WHERE THE WILD THINGS ARE!

I PRAISE YOU BECAUSE I AM FEARFULLY AND WONDERFULLY MADE; YOUR WORKS ARE WONDERFUL, I KNOW THAT FULL WELL.

—PSALM 139:14

EVERYBODY READY? GREAT!

Please be careful as you step onto the moving walkway. Make sure you hold the railing.

Take a good look around you, as this is the last time you'll see this building. Our tour is almost finished, and once it ends your personal journey as a misfit will begin.

This moving walkway will take us to our destination. Yeah, we could just walk there, but I didn't want to take any chances. In the past some people have gotten pretty shaken up and decided to turn back.

Please know this: There is no turning back from where we're headed.

I'm sure you're concerned about where we're headed, so let me begin the reveal by saying this destination is no picnic. In fact, it will be quite a struggle to get through it.

But as misfits we exist to face difficult situations and over-come them through God. While others take long vacations and ignore their life purposes, we roll up our sleeves and step up to the plate. We do more than merely expect oppo-sition—we confront it.

Misfits go where the Wild Things are!

One of the beauties of this misfit lifestyle is that regardless of your age, you can start affecting change in your world and in your areas of discomfort. Those around you will notice the leader in you and will follow and be inspired by you.

But don't be surprised to discover doubters either. People might say you're too bold or you're in way over your head, yet that's what separates us from them.

You're just like Max. In fact, you *are* Max!

Ahem—sorry. You may not know who Max is. Max is the main character in one of my favorite childhood stories. He's a free-spirited, imaginative young boy. And his story goes a little something like this:

Max is playing at home when he begins to imagine a land of "Wild Things" just across the sea. Being curious, as most little kids are, he decides to set sail for this land to see the Wild Things up close. When Max arrives on the other side of the sea, he finds himself face to face with some pretty scary monsters. They begin roaring and gnashing their teeth—yet this little boy isn't intimidated at all. Instead, he immediately approaches them, stretches out his hand, and tells the Wild Things to "Be still!" At that moment, they name Max "King of the Wild Things."

I know, I know—first Rudolph and now Max and the Wild Things. I'm a grown man, but this children's story has challenged me on levels I never would have expected.

The truth is that each of us can relate to Max.

WIRED FOR OUR OWN WILD THINGS

We also face "Wild Things" that can intimidate us—even prevent us from being all that we've been called to be. But I refuse, as should you, to let that happen in my life.

We need to have a childlike faith, just like Max, that can propel us forward and face to face with the Wild Things.

Part of the problem is that Christians don't fully understand or harness the power and authority they have in God.

God assigned character traits to each of us. And I believe God "wired" us with these specific and unique character traits according to the Wild Things that God wants each of us to take down.

So, the things that bother you? That cause you discomfort? That keep you up at night? They're probably not the same things that bother me—but that's okay. God designed *you* to deal with those particular Wild Things.

COURAGE

The one character trait we all need (and all share as Christians) in order to approach and face down each of our Wild Things is courage.

But what if you're a Christian and don't feel very courageous?

Well, it's not easy to show courage—especially when we need to. If that weren't true, then the world would be a very different place.

You might want to start by checking out Psalm 139. In this poem to God, David reminds us how much care and thought went into our individual creation. I'd like to believe that when David wrote this psalm, he was reflecting on his life and marveling at all God had done through him. David can't help but admit that he was "fearfully and wonderfully made."

To some people a statement like that may come across as boastful, but I'm pretty sure it was just another way of expressing worship to God for all God had done. And when you take all of that into account—especially how incredibly well God created each of us—the Wild Things in our lives may become less daunting. Why? Because now you know you were designed with purpose and precision—you're not a pile of junk.

The Message says this:

> Oh yes, you shaped me first inside, then out; you formed
> me in my mother's womb. I thank you, High God—
> you're breathtaking! Body and soul, I am marvelously
> made! I worship in adoration—what a creation! You
> know me inside and out, you know every bone in my
> body; you know exactly how I was made, bit by bit, how
> I was sculpted from nothing into something. Like an

open book, you watched me grow from conception to birth; all the stages of my life were spread out before you, the days of my life all prepared before I'd even lived one day. (Psalm 139:13–16)

DAVID AND GOLIATH

King David knew something about courage—and being divinely designed to conquer. In fact, David's claim to fame was defeating the Philistine giant, Goliath. Like Max, David was very young when he found himself facing the ultimate Wild Thing.

In 1 Samuel 17:4-7, we find a list of Goliath's attributes—attributes that made him a pretty intimidating figure. But in addition to Goliath, the entire Philistine army was present. They were considered the enemies of God, having already stolen the Ark of the Covenant and captured the Israelites.

Picture the scene: David, a young shepherd, brought lunch to his brothers on the battlefield. As he arrived in the valley, he saw the army of Israel shrinking in fear as Goliath and the Philistines threatened them.

Like most misfits, David didn't see this situation the way most people would. At that moment David was far more than uncomfortable—he was downright *offended!* So he confronted the army of Israel and told them that if they wouldn't take action, he *would*.

In true misfit form, David was compelled to walk in his authority, understanding that what he felt was righteous anger and it was to be acted on.

It wasn't long before word got back to King Saul about the bigmouthed shepherd boy. So Saul called for him. When David arrived, Saul told him how foolish he was for wanting to fight Goliath. Because David was only a boy and Goliath had been fighting since, like, forever, David wasn't considered for the battle.

Then David, boiling over with anger, boldly stepped up to King Saul and engaged him in conversation:

David said to Saul, "Let no one lose heart on account of this Philistine; your servant will go and fight him."

Saul replied, "You are not able to go out against this Philistine and fight him; you are little more than a boy, and he has been a warrior from his youth." (1 Samuel 17:32–33)

This was David's defining "misfit moment." He was probably having a mental conversation with himself, thinking over what the king had just said. Then David came to an incredible conclusion—it may have gone something like this:

> *If Goliath has been fighting since he was a boy, and since I'm a boy right now, then I'm starting pretty much on time. I'll start by slaying giants so that when I'm an adult, nothing will be too big or too wild for me to take down!*

David then looked straight into King Saul's eyes and said:

> I've been a shepherd, tending sheep for my father. Whenever a lion or bear came and took a lamb from the flock, I'd go after it, knock it down, and rescue the lamb. If it turned on me, I'd grab it by the throat, wring its neck,

and kill it. Lion or bear, it made no difference—I killed it. (1 Samuel 17:34–37 *The Message*)

And Saul replied, "Go. And GOD help you!" (1 Samuel 17:37 *The Message*).

Do you know what David did next? He went!

Why? Because that's what misfits do—we go. David is full of confidence and resolve. Plus he knows he isn't going alone.

It was now game time. As David prepared to fight Goliath, he tried on Saul's armor. Unfortunately the pieces didn't feel quite right, so David threw off the shield, helmet, and sword. Then he went to a nearby stream and picked up five smooth stones for his slingshot.

In part I believe David couldn't wear the king's armor or use his weapons because those tools weren't made for David. Instead, the future king of Israel had his own set of weapons that were perfect for him. Maybe they appeared inadequate in the hands of a young boy standing in the middle of a bloody battlefield. But they were David's weapons—and that made all the difference.

The lesson here is that your tools for battle won't be like your peers' tools—not even like your fellow misfits' tools. Sometimes they may appear "less than." What's important is that they're *your* tools—your weapons to slay the Wild Things that God has assigned to you.

Now back to the battle . . .

Think of the contrast between Goliath and David. Think about the taunts and warnings that rang in David's ears—yet not once did he flinch. He just walked into the middle of that field and approached Goliath, fully confident in what he was about to do. Goliath started laughing and taunting David—but David didn't back down. He decided to talk to Goliath, and he told the giant exactly how he was going to kill him:

> You come against me with sword and spear and javelin, but I come against you in the name of the LORD Almighty, the God of the armies of Israel, whom you have defied. This day the LORD will hand you into my hands, and I'll strike you down and cut off your head. This very day I will give the carcasses of the Philistine army to the birds of the air and the wild animals, and the whole world will know that there is a God in Israel. All those gathered here will know that it is not by sword or spear that the LORD saves; for the battle is the LORD's, and he will give all of you into our hands." (1 Samuel 17:45–47)

David's statement infuriated Goliath who started running toward David. No backing down now—not that David would have wanted to back down, anyway. Boldly, David also began running toward Goliath.

In mid-run David gripped the slingshot in his hand, swung it above his head, and released a stone toward the giant. It hit Goliath right between the eyes! It hit him so hard, in fact, that it sank into the giant's head.

Goliath was dead; the battle was over. David, like Max, had just tamed the wildest of all the Wild Things. A small slingshot defeated the unbeatable giant, and all because of the faith of a shepherd boy.

Think of the lives that were saved—the women, children, and the many men in battle—who would have otherwise fallen by the sword of the Philistines had David not acted with courage and conviction regarding the mission God planted in his heart.

In the same way, we can approach all the Wild Things in our path because the battle, ultimately, is God's to fight.

Later on in his life, this young shepherd boy would become king. But long before he was ever crowned, David had already proved he was fit to rule. He was designed for it, just as you're designed to fill your role here on earth—in this time and in this place. What are some of the "wild things" that you've had to face in your life? Do you sense that God placed them in your path for a reason? One of the hardest things for Christians to do—no matter how young or old they are—is using all of God's power at their disposal. And the Bible says there's a lot of it just ready to be harnessed. So . . . why do you suppose it's so hard to live day-by-day in that power? Do you consider yourself a courageous person? If so, can you recall specific instances where you had to use courage? If not, is it possible that you're not remembering times when you were courageous? What connection do you see, if any, between showing courage and harnessing God's power? Is it hard or easy for you to agree with the Bible that you have been "fearfully and wonderfully made" by God? If that's a difficult concept for you to accept, what would need to happen in your life to get you agreeing with that biblical truth—and living it out?

I pray you'll find the courage, like David did, to step up to the fight and not forget Who sent you to meet the moment of battle. No matter how your Wild Things taunt you, remember that you were designed—you were fearfully and wonderfully made by Almighty God—for that moment.

God knows that if he wants a Wild Thing taken down, he can rely on a misfit to do it.

Because misfits go where the Wild Things are.

And here we are—this is where we get off. Please watch your step.

CHAPTER 10

GO, MISFIT, GO!

"GO TO THE LOST, CONFUSED PEOPLE RIGHT HERE IN THE NEIGHBORHOOD. TELL THEM THAT THE KINGDOM IS HERE. BRING HEALTH TO THE SICK. RAISE THE DEAD. TOUCH THE UNTOUCHABLES . . . YOU HAVE BEEN TREATED GENEROUSLY, SO LIVE GENEROUSLY."

—MATTHEW 10:6–8 (*THE MESSAGE*)

AS YOU STEP OFF THE MOVING

walkway, you'll see a small waiting area—where the wait for our tour ends and your life mission begins.

Also notice the series of doors on either side of this waiting area. Gather around and allow me to explain what's behind each of these doors.

There's one door for each of you. But they aren't just any old doors; they are the Great Doors. I know they look pretty average and ordinary, but let's not judge them by their appearance. It's not about how the doors look or how they open; it's about *why* the door opens and *where* the door leads.

MORE ABOUT DOORS

Let's talk a little about doors—not the literal kind, but the figurative kind: The doors of opportunity. God will open doors for you, and God will also close doors that he doesn't want you to walk through. The important thing to understand is that no matter how great the opportunity seems, if God hasn't opened that door for you, leave it closed. God closed it for a reason.

But being typically stubborn and thoughtless at the worst possible times, we'd probably convince ourselves that *maybe* God made a mistake here. So we try to pry open the door. Sadly, even if we succeed at this little stunt, the broken-down door will always lead us nowhere.

God knows all that we're supposed to do for his name and what our hearts long for—even better than we *think* we do. In the book of Revelation, God tells us,

> "I know your deeds. See, I have placed before you an open door that no one can shut. I know that you have little strength, yet you have kept my word and have not denied my name." (Revelation 3:8)

Trust God and be secure in the promise that your door has already been prepared for you to step through.

But allow me to warn you about a few things before we go forward:

- First, it's easy to start believing the notion that, as we enter through our doors, we're truly achieving something. The reality is that we've yet to begin working! I've seen many men and women—who were entrusted with the great responsibility of representing God entirely—mess up their purposes because of unwise decisions.

• Second, as we move toward change, there is an enemy that wants to prevent us from affecting change. It will use all of our weaknesses to cripple us. So while we're out in the world taming Wild Things, we should first make sure that we're taming our sinful natures. And the way to do that is not to think we know best, but rather to allow God to take control:

"If you do what is right, will you not be accepted? But if you do not do what is right, sin is crouching at your door; it desires to have you, but you must master it." (Genesis 4:7)

MASTER SIN—OR IT WILL MASTER YOU

Take Judas Iscariot: He was part of one of the greatest ministries the world has ever seen. When he accepted the call of Jesus to join the disciples, Judas chose to walk through the door that Christ opened for him. Unfortunately for Judas, sin was waiting for him on the other side and, after a long pursuit, it mastered him.

I know you won't end up like Judas, but just remember to stay grounded in God's Word. Though my warning might raise feelings of discomfort in you, just know that beyond this wooden barrier is your pathway toward becoming an agent of change.

BACK TO THE DOORS

Now let's get to the business of these doors. You may be asking yourself, *Where exactly does that pathway lead?* Or *What does it look like?* Honestly, I don't really know—it looks different for each misfit. As you approach the threshold of the door, you won't see where your next step will land. You honestly have nothing to worry about, though—just step out.

As soon as you land, you must immediately get to work. And again, let me remind you that wherever you're headed will be in a state of chaos and need you to restore order to it. It longs for structure. Just follow God's direction and go.

The Bible tells us, "Your word is a lamp to my feet and a light for my path" (Psalm 119:105). Your steps won't be predictable; you'll have moments when you won't know what's next. But again, this is all part of the process; God designed it that way so we'd walk by faith, not by sight.

In Matthew 10:6–8, Jesus tells his disciples:

> "Go to the lost, confused people right here in the neighborhood. Tell them that the kingdom is here. Bring health to the sick. Raise the dead. Touch the untouchables. . . . You have been treated generously, so live generously." (*The Message*)

Keep in mind that right before Jesus instructed them to go out and become workers of the harvest, Jesus was accused of blasphemy for healing a paralytic man and forgiving his sins. (Matthew 9:1–8)

He also invited a tax collector named Matthew to join his ministry. But as Jesus and Matthew were sitting down to eat, a group of religious men came by to question Jesus about why he was eating with a tax collector. (Jewish culture looked down upon a rabbi eating with "those kinds of people.") (Matthew 9:9–13)

Later Jesus was questioned about fasting by some even-more religious men. (Matthew 9:14–17) While all of this was going on, Jesus was asked to bring a dead teenage girl back to life. (Matthew 9:18–19, 23–26) But on his way to perform that miracle, a woman who'd been sick for 12 years tugged at Jesus' robe—and she was immediately healed because of her faith. (Matthew 9:20–22)

Jesus then went on to heal two blind men. (Matthew 9:27–31) A mute demon-possessed man also found his way to Jesus and was healed. (Matthew 9:32–33) Yet, men who were far more religious attacked Jesus and accused him of being demon-possessed. (Matthew 9:34)

At this point Jesus realized that the work of healing the sick and saving the lost required *workers* to join him in his efforts!

I'm sure we can agree with the idea that Jesus could have done the work entirely on his own; but like everything Jesus did, there was always a lesson to be learned.

Jesus then decided to release his disciples to do the work of spreading the good news. (Matthew 10) Jesus understood that the only way to spread salvation was to build up other workers—so he gave them John the Baptist as an example to follow. (Matthew 11:1–19)

How many of you know who John the Baptist was?

John the Baptist preached the truth of God *before* Jesus started his ministry. John believed his calling was to prepare the way for the coming Messiah. In Matthew 11, Jesus boasted about John the Baptist, telling how he was persecuted—just as Jesus would be—for the sake of the gospel.

Jesus goes on to tell the disciples that the work will be exhausting, but that Jesus will also be there to rejuvenate them. God is always there to rejuvenate us when the work becomes exhausting. God doesn't tell us to take a break; God reminds us that he's there to renew our strength. Just as we are to pray, we should also work without ceasing.

Remember also that as we continue to work, we're to do so with confidence. Be sure to carry with you the same authority that David did. Without confidence, how would you approach the lost, the confused, the sickly, the dead, or even the untouchables? If you're supposed to reflect God, how can you do so while you're filled with insecurities?

Don't get me wrong; you'll have your moments of timidity and nervousness, but what we have to be careful of is not to let them take over our lives. When we allow God to work through us, our potential goes through the roof. We'll do things that never crossed our minds before, live experiences far beyond our expectations. Oh, the places you'll go! Let me also remind you that God has paved your way, working it all out for you in advance.

If you're wondering where to start in order to live out your misfit-ness, your neighborhood is probably your best bet in terms of bringing about change. Now is the appropriate time to do it; "the harvest is plentiful" (Matthew 9:37). Sin is always the biggest barrier to accomplishing all that God wants for us and becoming all that God wants us to be. Take some time and reflect on the sin areas of your life. Don't wallow in guilt about them—just reflect and when they come up, ask for Christ's forgiveness . . . then move on. We don't know how the stories of our lives will end—we don't even know what the next minute will bring! It's especially true for a Christian living out his or her misfit-ness to the fullest—God reserves the biggest thrill rides for you! Does that excite you . . . or is it an obstacle of fear you need to overcome? Since God can accomplish whatever he wants at any point—God truly doesn't require our assistance—is it hard for you sometimes to truly believe that God willingly includes us in his ministry to the world? (After all, our involvement has slowed progress down a lot!) What's the first thing you feel God leading you to do in your new life as a misfit?

Remember, you were built for this!

Wow, your door just opened. It's finally time to walk through it.

Just a word of advice: *When you walk through the Great Door, you'll end up in the same place you were when you accepted the misfit challenge—but this time your perspective will be entirely different.*

You came aboard this tour feeling uncomfortable, and you weren't really sure why or what to do about it. But now you're aware of your discomfort and are ready to take it on in all of your misfit-ness.

GO MISFIT, GO!

THE SOUNDTRACK

AVAILABLE ON I-TUNES, AMAZON, AND NAPSTER

FOR A FREE DOWNLOAD VISIT WWW.YOUTHEXPLOSION.COM